New Directions for
Higher Education

Betsy O. Barefoot
Jillian L. Kinzie
CO-EDITORS

Learning Analytics
in Higher Education

John Zilvinskis
Victor Borden
EDITORS

Number 179 • Fall 2017
Jossey-Bass
San Francisco

LB
525
.D84
No.
179

#1003194013

Learning Analytics in Higher Education
John Zilvinskis and Victor Borden
New Directions for Higher Education, no. 179
Co-editors: Betsy O. Barefoot and Jillian L. Kinzie

NEW DIRECTIONS FOR HIGHER EDUCATION, (Print ISSN: 0271-0560; Online ISSN: 1536-0741), is published quarterly by Wiley Subscription Services, Inc., a Wiley Company, 111 River St., Hoboken, NJ 07030-5774 USA.

Postmaster: Send all address changes to NEW DIRECTIONS FOR HIGHER EDUCATION, John Wiley & Sons Inc., C/O The Sheridan Press, PO Box 465, Hanover, PA 17331 USA.

Information for subscribers
New Directions for Higher Education is published in 4 issues per year. Institutional subscription prices for 2017 are:
Print & Online: US$454 (US), US$507 (Canada & Mexico), US$554 (Rest of World), €363 (Europe), £285 (UK). Prices are exclusive of tax. Asia-Pacific GST, Canadian GST/HST and European VAT will be applied at the appropriate rates. For more information on current tax rates, please go to www.wileyonlinelibrary.com/tax-vat. The price includes online access to the current and all online back files to January 1st 2013, where available. For other pricing options, including access information and terms and conditions, please visit www.wileyonlinelibrary.com/access.

Delivery Terms and Legal Title
Where the subscription price includes print issues and delivery is to the recipient's address, delivery terms are **Delivered at Place (DAP)**; the recipient is responsible for paying any import duty or taxes. Title to all issues transfers FOB our shipping point, freight prepaid. We will endeavour to fulfil claims for missing or damaged copies within six months of publication, within our reasonable discretion and subject to availability.

Back issues: Single issues from current and recent volumes are available at the current single issue price from cs-journals@wiley.com.

Disclaimer
The Publisher and Editors cannot be held responsible for errors or any consequences arising from the use of information contained in this journal; the views and opinions expressed do not necessarily reflect those of the Publisher and Editors, neither does the publication of advertisements constitute any endorsement by the Publisher and Editors of the products advertised.

Publisher: New Directions for Student Leadership is published by Wiley Periodicals, Inc., 350 Main St., Malden, MA 02148-5020.

Journal Customer Services: For ordering information, claims and any enquiry concerning your journal subscription please go to www.wileycustomerhelp.com/ask or contact your nearest office.
Americas: Email: cs-journals@wiley.com; Tel: +1 781 388 8598 or +1 800 835 6770 (toll free in the USA & Canada).
Europe, Middle East and Africa: Email: cs-journals@wiley.com; Tel: +44 (0) 1865 778315.
Asia Pacific: Email: cs-journals@wiley.com; Tel: +65 6511 8000.
Japan: For Japanese speaking support, Email: cs-japan@wiley.com.
Visit our Online Customer Help available in 7 languages at www.wileycustomerhelp.com/ask

Production Editor: Abha Mehta (email: abmehta@wiley.com).

Wiley's Corporate Citizenship initiative seeks to address the environmental, social, economic, and ethical challenges faced in our business and which are important to our diverse stakeholder groups. Since launching the initiative, we have focused on sharing our content with those in need, enhancing community philanthropy, reducing our carbon impact, creating global guidelines and best practices for paper use, establishing a vendor code of ethics, and engaging our colleagues and other stakeholders in our efforts. Follow our progress at www.wiley.com/go/citizenship

View this journal online at wileyonlinelibrary.com/journal/he

Wiley is a founding member of the UN-backed HINARI, AGORA, and OARE initiatives. They are now collectively known as Research4Life, making online scientific content available free or at nominal cost to researchers in developing countries. Please visit Wiley's Content Access - Corporate Citizenship site: http://www.wiley.com/WileyCDA/Section/id-390082.html

Printed in the USA by The Sheridan Group.

Address for Editorial Correspondence: Co-editors, Betsy Barefoot and Jillian L. Kinzie, New Directions for Higher Education, Email barefoot@jngi.org

Abstracting and Indexing Services
The Journal is indexed by Academic Search Alumni Edition (EBSCO Publishing); Higher Education Abstracts (Claremont Graduate University); MLA International Bibliography (MLA).

Cover design: Wiley
Cover Images: © Lava 4 images | Shutterstock

For submission instructions, subscription and all other information visit:
wileyonlinelibrary.com/journal/he

CONTENTS

Editors' Notes

For the last few years, we have been thinking and talking about the learning analytics phenomena with colleagues and each other, and watching passionate interest well up from disparate sources. We both attended several Learning Analytics & Knowledge (LAK) conferences hosted by the Society for Learning Analytics Research (SoLAR). When the conference was hosted in Indianapolis in 2014 a majority of the sessions featured computer scientists displaying successful predictive analytic programs; whereas at the 2016 conference in Edinburgh, Scotland, there was a push to emphasize the ways these projects measure the experience of learning. We have also noticed the last two or three annual forums of the Association for Institutional Research, a number of presentations regarding learning analytics, often with packed crowds of institutional research staff who have been tasked with contributing to the development of learning analytics on their campuses. We also noted that the Association for the Study of Higher Education Annual Conference has had a few sessions dedicated to learning analytics that have been attended by a small, yet dedicated, group.

In each of these experiences, we've noticed different *takes* on learning analytics from the scientist, higher education institution administrative staff, and scholar perspectives. Motivating our work is a question: "Why haven't learning analytics become prevalent within higher education?" Considering the ways technology has been incorporated within the academy over the past two decades (e-mail, websites, learning management systems), it would seem that learning analytics would be a natural evolutionary step—however, this hasn't happened at the pace or to the extent that we might have expected. In our research on the topic, we've noticed that the complexity of higher education as an enterprise, matched with required resources and understandings needed to successfully implement learning analytics, present immense challenges to incorporating these technologies effectively and productively.

Therefore, we conceptualized an issue of *New Directions for Higher Education* that would inform campus leaders, faculty, and staff about the scope and type of activities and initiatives required to bring learning analytics to their campus. The goal of this volume is to introduce the reader to a basic understanding of learning analytics and the types of projects and initiatives that several leading practitioners have adopted and adapted, providing substantive examples of implementation, and expert learnings on some of the more nuanced issues related to this topic.

New Directions for Higher Education, no. 179, Fall 2017   © 2017 Wiley Periodicals, Inc.
Published online in Wiley Online Library (wileyonlinelibrary.com) • DOI: 10.1002/he.20238

In the first chapter, we offer basic definitions of learning analytics, as well as an overview of *who* collaborates within learning analytics, exposing several broad issues for the reader to consider while reading the rest of the book. In the second chapter, Candace Thille reports findings from her and her colleagues' work with the Open Learning Initiative at Stanford University to inform the reader of the nuances of measuring student learning in digital environments, while describing the technology needed to achieve this feat and the assessment infrastructure required to improve teaching and learning in the digital environment.

Chapters 3 and 5 provide examples of developing learning analytics applications on the campuses of large universities. In Chapter 3, our colleagues from Indiana University (IU), Cathy Buyarski, Jim Murray, and Becky Torstrick, describe the implementation of learning analytics across the diverse campuses of IU, incorporating both an internally developed early warning system and externally developed (commercial) e-advising program. Steve Lonn, Timothy McKay, and Stephanie Teasley describe in Chapter 5 initiatives to create a culture of learning analytics at the University of Michigan through the development of symposia, grants, and faculty task forces.

In between these chapters, Matt Pistilli focuses on the key roles of feedback and intervention in virtually all types of learning analytics projects and initiatives. In Chapters 6 through 8, the authors explore several compelling issues related to learning analytics. John Fritz describes how and why including students, and promoting student responsibility for learning, is critical within learning analytics initiatives, based on his experiences at the University of Maryland, Baltimore County, as well as related efforts elsewhere. Jeffrey Johnson provides a rich analysis of issues related to ethics and justice that arise when working with student data generally as well as specifically with the types of applications now prevalent in the learning analytics realm. Chapter 8 presents findings from a national Office for Learning and Teaching–funded project in Australia that focuses on developing new thinking about how to characterize modern student experience that preserves the use of strong conceptual underpinnings that have historically guided research on student experience, and using analytics as a way to break the old molds and form new ones. In the final chapter, as the editors of the volume, we discuss some of the themes found within the issues, such as collaboration, interrogation, justice, and independence.

We believe that this volume can substantially inform readers who have been considering the implementation of learning analytics on their campus. However, we recognize that it is by no means comprehensive or complete, as new research and understandings are constantly emerging around this topic (just follow the comprehensive coverage by EDUCAUSE, SoLAR, and ACM); meanwhile, scholars within computer science, learning technologies, learning sciences, and education have contributed comprehensive understandings of learning analytics as a scholarly field (both

NEW DIRECTIONS FOR HIGHER EDUCATION • DOI: 10.1002/he

distinctions between *learning analytics, academic analytics, predictive analytics,* and *learner analytics,* relating to the level of analysis (student vs. class vs. curriculum), chronological characteristics of predictors (historical vs. contemporaneous), and type of outcomes (learning/behavior/development vs. retention/graduation); therefore, it is easy to see why newcomers find themselves uncertain when trying to specify the type of analytic project they wish to implement.

Distinguishing Learning Analytics Projects by Intended User. Learning analytics projects are often distinguished by the intended user or recipient of information. Previous work in analytics has led to the creation of tools to assist faculty with examining data from individual classes (Campbell et al., 2007). Chapters 2 and 5 in this volume have this focus. Other learning analytics projects primarily inform the work of academic advisors and other support staff with student guidance and coaching (Aguilar, Lonn, & Teasley, 2014; Barber & Sharkey, 2012). Chapters 3 and 4 fall into this category. Still other projects provide data directly to learners (Baker, 2007). Chapter 6 considers this target audience, at least in part. Analytics are also used to provide senior managers with management information related to teaching, learning, and student success (Buerck, 2014), which is also noted in Chapters 3 and 8. Regardless of the intended user, the chapters of this volume demonstrate that numerous campus partners must collaborate to implement a successful learning analytics project.

Relationship to Existing Roles and Functions

Implementation of learning analytics projects requires not only an understanding of the domain or the type of analytic project, but also an understanding of the amount of work and types of expertise needed. It is not feasible for even the most dedicated educators to create their own analytic systems. In addition to involving faculty as domain experts, information providers, and end-users, analytic project development often relies on collaboration among staff from several support units, such as centers for teaching and learning, student support services, institutional research, and information technology. Indeed, the development of learning analytics projects can change how these units routinely operate by providing opportunities for collaboration with new partners and new end-users. This may also lead to changes in the types of skillsets required for staff in these units.

Centers for Teaching and Learning.   Staff within a center for teaching and learning (CTL) or similarly named unit typically provide faculty development programs related to curriculum and course design and assessment. These units promote communities of practice around specific pedagogies (for example, service learning) and provide support for using new educational tools and technologies. CTL staff provide required expertise in instructional and pedagogical design for developing new capacity for learning analytics among faculty (Borden, Guan, & Zilvinskis, 2014).

Student Support Services. Educators serving in academic advising, student affairs, and supplemental instruction use traditional data sources (for example, advising records, student needs assessments, registrar information) to determine the most effective interventions to recommend to individual students, such as counseling, tutoring, and peer mentoring. These staff members typically adopt a holistic view of student life and development across the curriculum, cocurriculum, and extracurriculum. Student advising and support providers often have the most extensive experience in dealing with students directly as they formulate academic and life goals (Drake, 2011). When working in learning analytics, the expertise of these educators provides perspective regarding the complex relationship between in-class and out-of-class demands on student life, while also supplying an understanding of how learning analytics intervention can be coordinated throughout existing support systems and how existing systems need to be reshaped to accommodate learning analytics.

Institutional Research. Institutional research (IR) practitioners use theory-related concepts and knowledge of research design to frame research and guide interpretation, while providing aggregated information and analysis to senior managers. These professionals also help with the development of new reporting tools, some of which are dynamic reports or dashboards. When working in learning analytics, IR staff can apply their expertise in advancing interpretive models and conceptual frameworks for making sense of atheoretically based predictive analytics. Working on learning analytics projects requires IR staff to engage with colleagues who tend to use information in operational and individualized contexts rather than the more strategic and aggregate uses to which they are accustomed. In doing so, IR professionals can inform their colleagues about how measurement error qualifies the use of predictive analytics, making them much less precise than immediately apparent. Institutional researchers and other assessment professionals can also contribute by ensuring learning analytics projects include mechanisms for tracking the actions taken by staff and students in response to analytics information, to assess whether those actions are productive or counterproductive.

Information Technology. Information technology (IT) professionals implement systems, maintain data warehouses, secure infrastructures, establish data processes, and lead conversations about data governance. Furthermore, IT staff are experts when evaluating the feasibility of integrating new, commercial platforms within an institution's system. When working in learning analytics, IT staff serve as gatekeepers of data, but they also provide crucial guidance for the ways learning analytics projects can interact within current technologies and infrastructures.

Learning analytics brings together a variety of new ways to think about approaching the learning environment. Implementing learning analytics provides an opportunity to harness the expertise of existing roles (CTL, Student Services, IR, and IT) while also reshaping the work between these are paramount to successful implementation and long-term use of learning analytics.

Conclusion

The apparent absence of widespread, visible adoption of analytics among higher education institutions is befuddling to external observers who note the explosive growth in use of such techniques and tools in the for-profit goods and services sector. Colleges and universities appear to be well poised to adopt these technologies. They have complex, ongoing data collection and diagnostic systems. They have students who actively generate data with numerous behaviors online, consistently expanding their digital footprint. They have staffing infrastructure, like teaching and learning centers and assessment units, designated to measure and improve student learning. They have dedicated faculty members and advisors who share the goal with students of enhancing learning and degree completion. Vendors are willing to customize expensive technology, generating numerous products to achieve specific goals for distinct institution types, to support the learning analytics movement in higher education. As further incentive beyond the universal goal of excellence in teaching and learning, colleges and universities that successfully implement learning analytics to improve retention have the reward of enhanced revenue and improved prestige. It seems that with all of these available resources and incentives, learning analytics would be adopted naturally into the everyday life of students and educators alike.

On the other hand, there are many barriers to successful deployment of learning analytics projects within the higher education sector. Successful deployment of such systems requires an interdisciplinary effort that involves specialists in data management and visualization, educational research, and teaching and learning. Faculty members are crucial partners in both procuring course data for analysis and, ultimately, participating in interventions to improve the odds of student success. However, these potential partners are overloaded with the already demanding work of teaching, research, and service. Institutions of higher education have been slow to adopt broad assessments of student learning; accreditation agencies are just now moving beyond having institutions describe and measure success to requiring efforts to improve student learning. Furthermore, implementing learning analytics projects is expensive; efforts like these can require high-cost, cutting-edge technologies and hiring high-salaried, expert staff to manage these systems. Finally, the outcomes of higher education are very complex and multifaceted. Although seemingly a simplistic binary outcome, whether a student persists towards a degree is the net result of behaviors and circumstances related to performance across a range of classes; engagement and connection with other students, faculty, and staff within the institution; family obligations; personal relationship development; and personal finances. When applied to educational choices and behaviors, the kinds of decisions shaped by commercial analytics (for example, people who bought product X often bought product Y and Z), often seem trivial. More importantly, the hype generated by early instantiations of learning analytics have not been supported by clear evidence of effectiveness. The chapters of this volume reveal the complexity of deploying constructive analytic systems. Colleges and universities undoubtedly have the expertise and potential capacity for engaging constructively with learning analytics. However, successful deployment also requires a level of collaboration and systematic evaluation that challenges the inherently loosely coupled organizational systems that Weick (1976), Mintzberg (1979), and Cohen and March (1991) have argued fuel the creative capacity and disciplinary autonomy that underlie the core values and strengths of higher education institutions.

The near future of learning analytics is promising, and institutions can benefit from professors who have targeted interventions to improve student learning while preserving time for research. For institutions that weather rapidly changing funding options by ensuring successful retention of tuition money, learning analytics can harness data in a productive manner. However, underpinning these efforts and technologies is a clear vision and implementation strategy that navigates complex silos, research questions, sometimes conflicting leadership agendas, and, most importantly, a wide variety of student issues. Buy-in from a community with similar goals is critically necessary, and this buy-in must account for the specific culture, needs, and questions present at an individual institution.

References

Aguilar, S., Lonn, S., & Teasley, S. D. (2014). Perceptions and use of an early warning system during a higher education transition program. In *Proceedings of the Fourth International Conference on Learning Analytics and Knowledge* (pp. 113–117). New York, NY: ACM.

Baker, R. S. (2007). Modeling and understanding students' off-task behavior in intelligent tutoring systems. In *Proceedings of the SIGCHI Conference on Human Factors in Computing Systems* (pp. 1059–1068). New York, NY: ACM.

Barber, R., & Sharkey, M. (2012). Course correction: Using analytics to predict course success. In *Proceedings of the Second International Conference on Learning Analytics and Knowledge* (pp. 259–262). New York, NY: ACM.

Borden, V., Guan, K., & Zilvinskis, J. (2014). Learning analytics, IR, and assessment: Living together in the same house. Presented at the Association for Institutional Research 2014 Annual Forum, May 29. Orlando, FL.

Buerck, J. P. (2014). A resource-constrained approach to implementing analytics in an institution of higher education: An experience report. *Journal of Learning Analytics*, 1(1), 129–139.

Campbell, J. P., DeBlois, P. B., & Oblinger, D. G. (2007). Academic analytics: A new tool for a new era. *EDUCASE Review*, 42(4), 40–57.

Cohen, M. D., & March, J. G. (1991). Leadership in an organized anarchy. In M. W. Peterson, E. E. Chaffee, & T. H. White (Eds.), *ASHE reader on organization and governance in higher education* (4th ed.). Needham Heights, MA: Ginn Press.

Drake, J. K. (2011). The role of academic advising in student retention and persistence. *About Campus*, 16(3), 8–12.

Long, P., & Siemens, G. (2011). Penetrating the fog: Analytics in learning and education. *EDUCAUSE Review*, 46(5), 30–40.

Mintzberg, H. (1979). *The structuring of organizations*. Englewood Cliffs, NH: Prentice-Hall.

National Center for Education Statistics. (2017). College navigator: Rio Salado College. Retrieved from https://nces.ed.govcollegenavigator//?q=Rio±Salado±College&s=all&id=105668

Norris, D., Baer, L., Leonard, J., Pugliese, L., & Lefrere, P. (2008). Action analytics: Measuring and improving performance that matters in higher education. *EDUCAUSE Review*, 43(1), 42–44.

Parry, M. (2011, December 11). Colleges mine data to tailor students' experience. *The Chronicle of Higher Education*. Retrieved from https://chronicle.com/article/A-Moneyball-Approach-to/130062/

Simon, H. A. (1971). Designing organizations for an information rich world. In M. Greenberger (Ed.), *Computers, communications and the public interest* (pp. 37–67). Baltimore, MD: Johns Hopkins University Press. Retrieved from http://digitalcollections.library.cmu.edu/awweb/awarchive?type=file&item=33748

van Barneveld, A., Arnold, K. E., & Campbell, J. P. (2012). Analytics in higher education: Establishing a common language. *EDUCAUSE learning initiative*, 1(1), l-ll.

Weick, K. E. (1976). Educational organizations as loosely coupled systems. *Administrative Science Quarterly*, 21, 1–19.

DR. JOHN ZILVINSKIS *is an Assistant Professor of Student Affairs Administration at Binghamton University - State University of New York (SUNY).*

DR. JAMES WILLIS, III *is an independent scholar who has contributed articles in Educause and numerous chapters on the subject of learning analytics.*

DR. VICTOR BORDEN *is a Professor of Higher Education within the Department of Educational Leadership and Policy Studies at Indiana University Bloomington.*

2

This chapter describes an open learning analytics system focused on learning process measures and designed to engage instructors and students in an evidence-informed decision-making process to improve learning.

Incorporating Learning Analytics in the Classroom

Candace Thille, Dawn Zimmaro

Technology-mediated learning environments enable us to capture data from learners' interactions and use those data to drive powerful feedback loops to instructors, students, course designers, and the science of learning. However, learning analytics tend to focus on metrics that are proxies for student learning—from click stream data such as number of logins and time spent viewing a webpage or videos to more macro measures such as course grades and graduation rates. In this chapter, we discuss the successes, challenges, and promise of implementing a learning analytics system that focuses on learning process measures. Specifically, we address the following issues: How do we create effective learning and assessment opportunities to generate meaningful data? Once we have those data, how do we create open and accessible models that predict and explain student progress toward learning objectives? How do we support instructors and students in making meaningful data-driven decisions to inform and improve learning and teaching opportunities? What organizational structures are needed for learning analytics to support a virtuous cycle of continuous improvement? Our goal in this chapter is to demonstrate how we can use an integrated learning analytics system to engage instructors and students in an evidence-informed decision-making process to improve learning.

Introduction

In the first chapter the authors define learning analytics as "the process of using live data collected to predict student success, promoting intervention or support based on those predictions and monitoring the influence of that action." In the current chapter, we focus on an approach to predicting student success and how those predictions can be used to inform

New Directions for Higher Education, no. 179, Fall 2017 © 2017 Wiley Periodicals, Inc.
Published online in Wiley Online Library (wileyonlinelibrary.com) • DOI: 10.1002/he.20240

evidence-informed teaching practices. Additionally, we argue that in order to effectively support improvement in teaching and learning, institutions of higher education should not outsource the design and development of analytics systems. Lastly, we argue that transparency and openness in course design, data modeling, and research in learning analytics is critical to effectively supporting evidence-informed teaching practices.

Appropriately instrumented online learning environments afford us the ability to capture data about learners' interactions and use those data to drive powerful feedback loops to instructors, students, course designers, and the science of learning. However, most learning analytics systems tend to focus on event data or performance data metrics that may be reasonable predictors for student retention but not for student learning. Event data capture elements such as number of logins, time spent per page, and clickstream logs. Performance data focuses on measures such as percent correct, course grades, and course completion rates. Early alert systems, typically instantiated as dashboards for instructors or advisors, are increasingly being used, but the metrics that determine students' alert status are generated by fairly simplistic student models (for example, login counts and course averages) and do not provide specific information about how to address the students' learning difficulties.

At the Open Learning Initiative (OLI) at Stanford we have developed an integrated learning analytics system that focuses on capturing not just event or performance data but rather student learning process data. *Learning process data* refers to data generated from student interactions with a task or assessment that records not only the students' final result but also the processes that students use when solving a problem. In this chapter, we discuss the successes and challenges of implementing a learning analytics system that focuses on student learning process data, and how we can use analytics to engage instructors and students in an evidence-informed decision-making process to improve learning.

The Open Learning Initiative Approach to Learning Analytics

Our primary mission and focus is grounded in a theory of change best articulated by Herbert Simon in 1998 (and modified slightly by us as shown parenthetically in the following quote): "Improvement in post-secondary education will require converting teaching (and courseware and learning analytic system development) from a solo sport to a community based research activity." We engage faculty and institutional partners not as consumers or users but rather as collaborators in research and development. The output of our collaborative processes is courseware that is designed to simultaneously improve student learning while contributing to our shared fundamental understanding of human learning. Recent advances in neuroscience, cognitive science, computer science, and data science set the foundation for rapid progress in the science of human learning; however, the

NEW DIRECTIONS FOR HIGHER EDUCATION • DOI: 10.1002/he

results of research have historically not translated into successful changes in teaching practice or student learning. OLI provides a model for using educational technology to shift the relationship of learning research and teaching practice in service of improving student learning.

The OLI course design process starts with the domain experts and learning engineers developing a skills map. The skills map is an articulation of learning objectives and the skills that those objectives comprise. Learning objectives specify what students will be able to do or know at the end of a section of instructional content. A skill identifies the discrete concept, or knowledge component, embedded within the learning objective. Each learning objective comprises one or more skills. Interactive activities and quizzes are created to assess students' learning related to the various skills identified in the skills map. OLI's theoretical learning model links to the skills map to predict student mastery of each skill and related learning objectives. Analytics from these learning models are then presented in a dashboard display for instructors, and in more limited form, for students (Bier, Lip, Strader, Thille, & Zimmaro, 2014).

We are currently developing a platform-independent, open analytics system called the Open Analytics Research Service (OARS). OARS gives instructors, course designers, and researchers the ability to review and modify the skills map and the learning model. In the first iteration of OARS, the interface allows instructors or researchers to choose the predictive model, initially a Bayesian Knowledge Tracing model, and the system is designed to expand to include additional models. OARS dynamically analyzes the data produced by student activity in the OLI courseware in real time. The Instructor Dashboard presents the instructor with an estimate of student learning at any point in time for each learning objective in the course. The learning estimate predicts the likelihood that a student would be able to respond correctly to previously unseen problems or questions assessing a specific learning objective. Faculty can use the Instructor Dashboard to identify students who may be struggling and, based on the insight gleaned from the dashboard, provide recommendations or instructional interventions. The Instructor Dashboard also supports faculty to identify learning objectives that the majority of the class has yet to master. See Figures 2.1 and 2.2 for examples of data visualizations included in the Instructor Dashboard.

While there is increasing interest in personalized and adaptive learning systems, there is also increasing concern about the lack of transparency and peer review in the academic decision making that these external systems represent. Institutions and faculty are becoming increasingly concerned about loss of control of their core decision making about teaching and learning.

The data that are collected from the student interactions in adaptive learning systems are modeled and used for pedagogical decision making, either so the system can make autonomous decisions (for example, select a learning task for the student) or to give information to the instructor to

Figure 2.1. Example learning objective and the number of students who are predicted to have mastered this objective

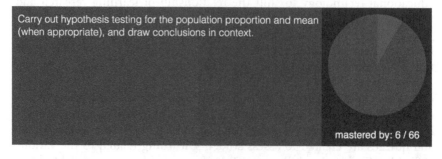

Figure 2.2. Example skill and the distribution of learners who have mastered and not mastered the skill by number of activity attempts (unique activities related to the skill)

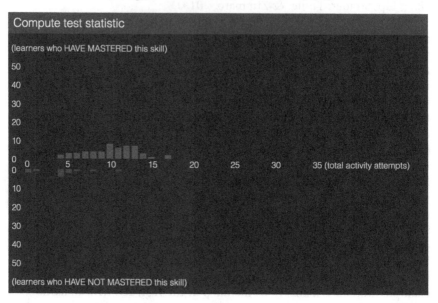

support their decision making (for example, present a visual representation of a student's predicted competence on specified learning objectives). Current machine learning algorithms, modeling on the data generated by student interactions, are powerful for making predictions but not for generating explanations. This limits their capacity to support transparent pedagogical decision making.

The OARS system offers an alternative and transparent approach to engaging in use of effective adaptive and personalized learning systems.

Figure 2.3. Open Analytics Service (OARS) Components

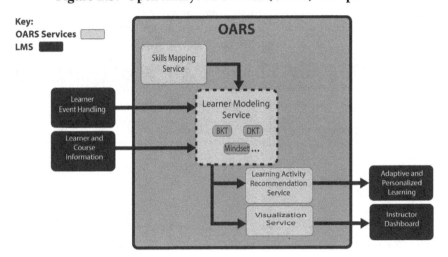

The OARS services, which are external to a learning management system (LMS), are designed to be flexible enough to support different tagging, modeling, and visualization approaches across various LMS platforms and courses as shown in Figure 2.3. For example, the skills mapping service supports OLI's tagging schema (resources to skills and skills to learning objectives), but it can support different schema as well. For example, if an instructor/researcher wanted to tag resources with "resource type" (for example, text, video, discussion, problem) and model whether student time spent using different resources changed outcomes, the tagging could be changed in the skills mapping service and the predictive model could be changed in the learner modeling service to account for "time spent" as a measure rather than "problem correctness."

Creating Opportunities to Generate Meaningful Data

While much attention by other online course designers has been given to elements such as video length, content layout, graphics and visualizations, and how to predict various persistence outcomes, relatively little attention has been given to the measures of student learning. Much time has been spent on the technological inputs and data outputs of online courses, while ignoring the assessments that bind the course content and activities to the data generated from student interactions with the course.

Any assessment, and the data derived from it, is an inexact measure of the learning that occurs. Learning analytics has often focused on event and performance data measures, while often not capturing learning process data that may contain better approximations of learning. Event data capture elements such as number of logins, time spent per page,

NEW DIRECTIONS FOR HIGHER EDUCATION • DOI: 10.1002/he

Figure 2.4. Example assessment activity that connects to the skill (Compute Test Statistic) and learning objective (Carry out hypothesis testing for the population proportion and mean (when appropriate), and draw conclusions in context)

SCENARIO: PART-TIME COLLEGE STUDENTS BY GENDER

Consider the population of part-time college students. Suppose that 60% of this population is female.

Here is the sampling distribution for the proportion of females in random samples of n students. The standard deviation is approximately 0.10. Lines indicate a distance of 1 and 2 standard deviations above and below the mean.

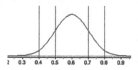

Learn By Doing
(1 point possible)
Use the graph to approximate the test statistic if p̂ = 0.75:

[   ]   ?

[ ]

SUBMIT   HINT

and clickstream logs. Performance data focuses on measures such as percent correct and course completion rates. Learning process data is derived from assessments linked to specific skills/knowledge components, with an example shown in Figure 2.4 above. In creating activities, exercises, and assessments, we align to learning process objectives that reflect the kind of learning we want to capture. The predictions we make from these assessments are only as good as the quality of the measurements we make.

As Grant Wiggins (1997) wrote, "It's not teaching that causes learning. Attempts by the learner to perform cause learning, dependent upon the quality of feedback and opportunities to use it" (p. 7). Our assessments contain the two critical elements as highlighted by Wiggins. They provide goal-directed practice where learners work toward a specific level of performance and continually monitor their performance relative to clearly defined goals. Additionally, assessments provide feedback that explicitly relates students' performance to the criteria. The feedback is timely, frequent, and constructive, and students are given opportunities to incorporate that feedback into further practice.

The data collected from technology-mediated learning environments can provide a detailed record of the students' learning process, making that process amenable to scientific study. We design a range of tasks—grounded in current theories of human learning—that structure performances, automatically collecting enough pieces of evidence that can be identified and aggregated to provide a reasonably coherent picture of the learners' knowledge state and of the learning process.

The assessment tasks we design must have construct-validity evidence to be effective measures of the skills we are trying to model. Construct validity includes evidence of content relevance, representativeness, and technical quality (Messick, 1989). Messick (1994) described a key issue for the content aspect of construct validity, which is determining the knowledge, skills, attitudes, motives, and other attributes to be revealed by the assessment task; establishing content relevance can be accomplished by conducting a task analysis or curriculum analysis. Similar to Messick, Embretson (1983) also supported the use of cognitive-process analysis or research to determine the mechanisms underlying task performance as a method to determine construct validity. This involves breaking down the task into requisite component processes and assembling them into a functional theory.

However, as Messick (1994) articulated, it is not sufficient to design assessment tasks that are relevant to the construct (or content) domain. The assessment task should be representative of the content but also the underlying processes in a domain. For example, a statistician might not only calculate measures of central tendency such as mean, median, and mode, but would use those measures to determine the representativeness of a sample drawn from a population. Therefore, assessment tasks should not only focus on having learners calculate measures of central tendency but also apply them in context. Ensuring that assessment tasks have evidence of content relevance and representativeness, as appraised by expert professional judgment, serves to address the content aspect of construct validity.

Moss, Girard, and Haniford (2006) cited a National Research Council (NRC) report, "Knowing What Students Know," that called for an approach to assessment that would "be largely determined by a model of cognition and learning that describes how people represent knowledge and develop competence in the domain." In particular, authors of the NRC suggest that assessments should "[address] learners' knowledge structures, metacognition, problem-solving strategies, progress along a domain-specific developmental continuum, transfer of knowledge and skills to problems in multiple contexts, and communicative practices in the domain" (p. 124). Assessments that are designed in this way help to make students' thinking visible to instructors and to themselves, provide timely and informative feedback that supports learning, and demonstrate students' learning progress (Moss et al., 2006).

OLI conducts cognitive task analyses with content experts to make the underlying skills and processes explicit. Content experts, learning scientists, and assessment experts collaborate on the design of assessment tasks that allow students to demonstrate those skills. The tasks range from selected-response questions that help to support and scaffold a student's learning by providing answer choices and feedback targeted at student misconceptions to constructed-response questions that require students to integrate and synthesize their learning across multiple skills.

The learning environments that we have historically built in OLI supported learners to engage in computer-mediated individual tasks. Technology now mediates the interactions of learners in a social context so the data we now collect also measures and supports the learners' participation in learning activities within a larger community of practice. In addition to collecting data that support inferences about the learner's trajectory in the development of individual cognitive skills, we can also collect data that support inferences about the learner's trajectory in development of identity and roles within a group.

As technology-mediated learning environments continue to evolve, our ability to design assessment tasks that more accurately capture student learning will also evolve. As Moss et al. (2006) state, "Evolving conceptions of learning and studies of how evidence of learning is actually used are pushing our conceptions of what assessment is and what validity theory needs to accomplish" (p. 122).

Creating Open and Accessible Predictive and Explanatory Models

Several advances in computer science are revolutionizing other fields and are fueling interest in using technology not only to provide greater access to education but also to transform instruction. Foremost among them is the maturing of machine learning—the study and construction of algorithms that can learn from and make predictions on data. Computer scientists have made progress in designing learning algorithms to work with extremely large data sets and build models. A branch of machine learning, reinforcement learning, is a framework that shifts the focus of machine learning from simple pattern recognition to experience-driven sequential decision making. Recurrent neural networks, also called "deep learning," belong to a class of dynamic models that connect artificial neurons over time. The use of recurrent neural networks has rapidly advanced progress on several time series tasks, such as speech recognition and image captioning (LeCun, Bengio, & Hinton, 2015). Learning researchers and computer scientists are currently debating the value of deep learning for tracing human knowledge development (Khajah, Lindsey, & Mozer, 2016; Piech et al., 2015). The OARS system supports research that improves knowledge modeling.

The large data sets generated by use of educational technologies by thousands of students in thousands of contexts, combined with new

NEW DIRECTIONS FOR HIGHER EDUCATION • DOI: 10.1002/he

machine learning algorithms, provide an unprecedented opportunity to discover new patterns that are predictive of student success. Given that we know that instructional methods can be differentially effective for different groups and individuals in different contexts, it is important that the models are trained on representative populations in multiple contexts. It is also problematic if the models are trained on data resulting from unconscious biases (e.g., gender, class, and/or racial bias) that influenced the outcome decisions. If models are not critically evaluated before they are used to inform the design of learning environments, we run the risk of building tools to reinforce existing norms that reproduce inequality.

Currently, the selected-response questions that include hints and feedback and are scored correct/incorrect drive our prediction models. These data are derived from assessments that are designed to evaluate students' thinking and learning as it pertains to specific skills. The assessments contain answer choices that target student misconceptions, provide immediate feedback that addresses the rationale behind the correct answer or specific misconception, and progressively scaffold students' learning of interrelated skills. The assessments are embedded frequently throughout OLI courses, allowing students multiple practice opportunities. The kinds of data we collect and the frequency with which we collect the data allow us to engage in the type of student-level, learning process–based analytics that provide not only predictive models but also explanatory models. As technologies and modeling capabilities evolve, we will include data from open-ended questions in our algorithms.

Our long-term goal is to create an open analytics system that allows any course, delivered on a platform that supports tagging resources with learning objectives and skills, to connect to the skills mapping, learner models, and data visualizations. The learner models are openly available and modifiable to allow for iterative improvement and research on the models.

The systems and algorithms used to model the data are not neutral. Any system built using data will reflect the biases and decisions made when collecting that data, as well as the behaviors and judgments of the groups and individuals from whom the data are collected. Within education, there is evidence that diverse populations must be used to develop detectors because not all models work for all students even when overall model quality is high (cf. Ocumpaugh, Baker, Gowda, Heffernan, & Heffernan, 2014). There are multiple examples from other sectors showing the negative impact of systems built on biased or unrepresentative data.

Higher education has the opportunity to use research in human learning, large data sets, data mining, data modeling, and the design of reporting systems to detect and counterbalance unconscious implicit biases. For example, mining of large data sets in one study already has revealed that significant gendered performance differences are ubiquitous in large introductory STEM lecture courses. This has led to the hypothesis that evaluation methods used in STEM lecture courses interact with stereotype threat to create gendered performance differences (Koester, Grom, & McKay, 2016). If models are not transparent and critically evaluated before they are built into predictions systems, data mining and the resulting decision support systems will simply reproduce existing patterns, inherit the prejudice of prior decision makers, and further entrench biases in the education system. The tools also have the potential to provide greater transparency that may be used to detect and reduce human bias.

Supporting Evidence-Informed Decision Making

Instructors are often faced with a myriad of information and data about their students' learning. Discerning how to sort through and use these data to make decisions about just-in-time changes to teaching can be a daunting task. The key to supporting instructors in using these data is to provide the data and related visualizations in consumable form that provide suggestions and recommendations for action and interventions.

The OARS system provides instructors with data visualizations that summarize class and individual student mastery of skills and learning objectives. Instructors receive information about the probability that a given student has learned a given learning objective, comprising several skills. Data visualizations are used to demonstrate how well an entire class or an individual student has mastered the learning objectives in the course. These visualizations display the number and percent of students that have mastered or not yet mastered the learning objectives contained within a given module. We have delineated two levels of mastery: "mastered" and "not mastered." We believe that this two-tiered approach provides the most meaningful and actionable interpretation of student performance. Students who have "mastered" a learning objective or skill are predicted to have sufficiently learned the concept. Students who have "not mastered" a learning objective or skill require additional support. Instructors can view details about the specific skills by class or individual to identify where additional support is needed. Some analytics systems report multiple levels of mastery creating a false sense of precision in models that are not yet able to truly provide that level of accuracy.

Data is limited on how faculty are interpreting the visualizations and how their interpretations are informing their decision making. Evaluations of instructor dashboards tend to focus on how useful and easy to use the dashboards are, with few evaluations exploring how dashboards can help instructors improve teaching or student learning and performance. In order for the visualizations and feedback tools to support decision making, dashboards must be easy to use for those who have limited data analysis and visualization skills (Ginda, Suri, Bueckle, & Börner, 2016).

Our goal is to design learning analytics feedback tools (i.e., dashboards) for instructors that enable them to improve their pedagogical approach. We are continuing to explore how instructors interpret existing dashboards, how the interpretations the dashboard enables supports (or conflicts with) their teaching goals, and how intentionally selective displays of information may influence pedagogical decision making.

In addition to instructor dashboards, the use of student feedback tools and dashboards is also an area for further exploration. Corrin and de Barba (2015) found that students generally are able to use learning analytics dashboards to identify gaps in their actual and expected performance and to use that information to make changes to their study strategies. However, their evidence suggests that students were unable to connect the dashboard feedback to their current learning strategies. In the future, we plan for the OARS system to provide real-time student feedback tools that encourage students to identify areas where they have yet to master the learning objectives and to use that feedback to inform their learning processes.

Implementing a Continuous Improvement Cycle

Supporting individual instructors to use learning analytics to engage in evidence-informed teaching practices is a challenge in and of itself, but without larger organizational structures in place to support these types of pedagogical changes, the impact on the teaching and learning process may be small. Higher education institutions need to locally invest in and support the technological and pedagogical shifts needed to create a culture of using learning analytics as part of a continuous improvement cycle. One such investment that we advocated for earlier in this chapter is putting resources into creating research and development partnerships that support intra- and interinstitutional collaborations around learning analytics rather than outsourcing development to external vendors. Outsourced solutions typically involve closed proprietary modeling systems, which reflect the values and biases of the designer or the biases in the data on which the models were trained.

Personalized and adaptive educational technologies have great potential for good, but there is also potential for harm if careful, rigorous thought is not devoted to understanding the learning process, specifying the learning process objective of interest, designing how and from whom the data are collected, and choosing how data are modeled and represented. Collaborations to develop such technologies must be grounded in transparency and openness in course design and data modeling to be able to effectively support evidence-informed teaching practices. The OARS system is designed to support such transparency and openness. We work within and across institutions to support collaborations around course design, analytics, and research so that changes and improvements are not isolated to a single instructor but rather are shared across the larger development and research community.

In an issue brief by the U.S. Department of Education's Office of Educational Technology (Bienkowski, Feng, & Means, 2012), the authors identified several limitations in institutional capacity related to effectively using learning analytics: technical challenges related to collecting, storing, and sharing data; infrastructure costs in terms of hardware, software, and human resources; usability of dashboards and other data feedback reports for instructors and students; and potential biases in how results are interpreted. These challenges are applicable to not only large, institutional-level data mining and learning analytics efforts but also to learning process–level analytics. If the learning analytics system does not integrate with other institutional data systems, instructors may face technical and infrastructural challenges in using the system in their teaching. Additionally, instructors may need support in terms of local staff to help integrate this system with existing teaching tools. Lastly, instructors will need training in how to use data from learning analytics systems to inform just-in-time changes to their teaching practices and how to support their students' learning. This requires a shift in use of analytics from using data for reporting and accountability to using data for continuous improvement. As Bienkowski et al. (2012) suggest, "successful application of educational data mining and learning analytics will not come without effort, cost, and a change in educational culture to more frequent use of data to make decisions" (p. 37).

Summary

Our work at OLI, including the OARS system, is centered on creating an integrated learning analytics system to engage instructors and students in an evidence-informed decision-making process to improve learning. The foundation of this system is creating effective learning and assessment tasks grounded in cognitive and sociocultural perspectives, and using learning process data derived from those tasks to drive open and transparent prediction and explanatory models. The output of these models are powerful feedback loops to instructors, students, course designers, and the science of learning. Research on how to best support instructors and students, both individually and at the institutional level, in making decisions based on these data and visualizations is still evolving. The long-term hope is that classroom-based learning analytics developed and implemented as part of community-based research collaborations across higher education institutions will significantly change practice in the teaching-learning continuum.

References

Bienkowski, M., Feng, M., & Means, B. (2012). *Enhancing teaching and learning through educational data mining and learning analytics: An issue brief.* Washington, DC: U.S. Department of Education, Office of Educational Technology.

Bier, N., Lip, S., Strader, R., Thille, C. & Zimmaro, D. (2014). An approach to knowl-edge component / skill modeling in online courses. *Open Learning*. Retrieved from https://static1.squarespace.com/static/5330c47be4b03ea35b2645a8/t/5361cb4be4b0 c9d8aaa7d3be/1398917963378/AnApproachtoSkillMappinginOnlineCourses043020 14.pdf

Corrin, L., & de Barba, P. (2015). How do students interpret feedback delivered via dash-boards? In P. Blikstein, A. Merceron, & G. Siemens (Eds.), *Proceedings of the 5th In-ternational Conference on Learning Analytics and Knowledge* (pp. 430–431). New York, NY: ACM.

Embretson, S. E. (1983). Construct validity: Construct representation versus nomothetic span. *Psychological Bulletin, 93*, 179–197.

Ginda, M., Suri, N., Bueckle, A., & Börner, K. (2016). Empowering instructors in learn-ing management systems: Interactive heat map analytics dashboard. Retrieved from cns.iu.edu/docs/publications/2016-ginda-emporing-instructors-LAK.pdf

Khajah, M., Lindsey, R. V., & Mozer, M. C. (2016). How deep is knowledge tracing? In T. Barnes, M. Chi, & M. Feng (Eds.), *Proceedings of the Ninth International Conference on Educational Data Mining* (pp. 94–101). Raleigh, NC: Educational Data Mining Society Press.

Koester, B., Grom, G., & McKay, T. (2016). Patterns of gendered performance differ-ences in introductory STEM courses. Submitted to PLoS One. https://arxiv.org/abs/ 1608.07565

LeCun, Y., Bengio, Y., & Hinton, G. (2015). Deep learning. *Nature, 521*(7553), 436–444.

Messick, S. (1989). Validity. In R. L. Linn (Ed.), *Educational measurement* (3rd ed., pp. 13–103). New York, NY: Macmillan.

Messick, S. (1994). Validity of psychological assessment: Validation of inferences from persons' responses and performances as scientific inquiry into score meaning. *American Psychologist, 50*, 741–749.

Moss, P. A., Girard, B. J., & Haniford, L. C. (2006). Validity in educational assessment. *Review of Research in Education, 30*, 109–162.

Ocumpaugh, J., Baker, R., Gowda, S., Heffernan, N., & Heffernan, C. (2014). Population validity for educational data mining models: A case study in affect detection. *British Journal of Educational Technology, 45*(3), 487–501.

Piech, C., Bassen, J., Huang, J., Ganguli, S., Sahami, M., Guibas, L., & Sohl-Dickstein, J. (2015). *Deep knowledge tracing*. Retrieved from https://web.stanford.edu/~cpiech /bio/papers/deepKnowledgeTracing.pdf

Simon, H. (1998). *Teaching: Need it be a solo sport?* [Videorecording]. Delivered at Last Lecture Series, Carnegie Mellon University, Pittsburgh, PA.

Wiggins, G. (1997). Feedback: How learning occurs. *AAHE Bulletin, 50*(3), 7–8.

CANDACE THILLE *is an assistant professor in the Graduate School of Education and the executive director of the Open Learning Initiative, Stanford University.*

DAWN ZIMMARO *is the director of learning design and assessment at the Open Learning Initiative, Stanford University.*

This chapter explores lessons learned from two different learning analytics efforts at a large, public, multicampus university—one internally developed and one vended platform. It raises questions about how to best use analytics to support students while keeping students responsible for their own learning and success.

3

Learning Analytics Across a Statewide System

Catherine Buyarski, Jim Murray, Rebecca Torstrick

Learning analytic efforts are fundamentally reshaping how colleges and universities think about student success. With student learning, achievement, and retention at the forefront of institutional efforts to meet completion goals, learning analytic efforts at Indiana University have allowed campuses to reengineer systems and interventions to ensure that students graduate. This chapter reflects on the implementation of two learning analytic projects that are both part of technological application initiatives called Integrated Planning and Advising Services (IPAS) (Wagner & Longanecker, 2016). One is an institutionally developed alert system; the other is a vendor-delivered platform that provides predictive analytics, in addition to best practices guidance based on data from over 170 participating institutions. While learning analytics projects may be initiated at any level, Indiana University chose to implement these projects at the system level. This approach allowed the seven-campus university to leverage the resources that are required with any learning analytics project to ensure that all campuses benefitted. Further, the systems attempted to provide benefits to campus decision makers, faculty, and student service staff alike so that student success initiatives were supported at all levels of each campus.

Many institutions are focusing time, attention, and resources on projects and strategies designed to increase student retention and graduation. For Tinto and Pusser (2006), a key institutional condition for student success is regular feedback including monitoring, assessing, and communicating student performance through mechanisms such as early alert systems. These systems "provide a formal, proactive feedback structure through which university faculty alert students and their campus support agents to issues impacting academic performance" (Faulconer, Geissler,

New Directions for Higher Education, no. 179, Fall 2017 © 2017 Wiley Periodicals, Inc.
Published online in Wiley Online Library (wileyonlinelibrary.com) • DOI: 10.1002/he.20241

33

Majewski, & Trifilo, 2014, p. 45). While predictive models look at preentry attributes of students in an effort to evaluate risk, early alert systems identify needy students once they exhibit behaviors that put them at risk for course failure or withdrawal (Cuseo, 2006; Davidson, Beck, & Mulligan, 2009). Early alert systems help address the common issue of students not knowing if they are doing well in a course until it is too late to make changes, thus allowing institutions to identify and direct support services to those students who are most in need (Pistilli & Arnold, 2010).

Midterm grades, often the first feedback students receive about class performance, arrive too late to allow many students to adjust to improve class performance. Robust early alert systems, providing specific, behavior-oriented feedback and linking students with appropriate interventions, can be far more effective toward these ends (Cuseo, 2006; Simmons, 2011). Such systems often track issues ranging from attendance to classroom behaviors to psychosocial issues like adjustment to college or mental health (Tampke, 2013). Systems can include case management and reporting, notetaking capabilities, and student appointment scheduling (Faulconer et al., 2014). Early alert systems have been used to identify specific issues such as attendance (Bowen, Price, Lloyd, & Thomas, 2005; Chappel, 2010; Hudson, 2005), target specific student populations (Lonn, Krumm, Waddington, & Teasley, 2012), and drive students to support services such as tutoring (Cai, Lewis, & Hidgon, 2015). Campuses that employ early alert systems as a method for enhancing student success report moderate to great satisfaction with them (Simmons, 2011).

Learning analytics data is most valuable when it guides interventions that link specific students to appropriate supports at the time of need. In fact, "predictions that are not linked to treatments that have been shown to make a difference for diagnosed risk are empty exercises" (Wagner & Longanecker, 2016, p. 57). Learning analytics, whose goal is supporting student retention and graduation, need to be embraced at all levels of the institution from top leadership to the faculty, advisors, and staff who will use the data to intervene with students.

Because successful use of learning analytics requires engagement across the institution, relevant stakeholders must be involved from the beginning in the design of the system. Tampke (2013) described a process that facilitated consensus building around three main issues: (1) initiating alerts, (2) what would evoke an alert, and (3) interventions. Critical to the implementation of learning analytics are issues of organizational capacity in terms of getting analytics tools into the hands of all relevant persons as well as ensuring services and supports are available to students with risk factors (Lonn et al., 2012).

Among stakeholders, learning analytic programs succeed when they have the support of the faculty and staff who will report and/or intervene based on appropriate data. Most campuses have volumes of information about student success but end users can be left to sort through potentially hundreds of data points to find both meaningful and actionable items (Bach, 2010). Creating and using such data is enhanced when reporting, access, and intervention strategies are streamlined and made convenient for faculty and staff (Cuseo, 2006). Faulconer et al. (2014) found that faculty are most likely to participate in analytics-driven interventions when they believed that indicators of poor performance were the first step in starting conversations with students who were unlikely to interact with instructors. Other key components to using analytics to enhance student success include faculty and staff development on the use and interpretation of data as well as incentives and rewards for participation (Cuseo, 2006; Tinto & Pusser, 2006; Wagner & Ice, 2012). All of these components are required in successful implementation of learning analytics.

Learning Analytic Implementation at Indiana University

Indiana University is a very large, multicampus public university, grounded in the liberal arts and sciences, and a world leader in professional, medical, and technological education. Within the overarching university structure, Indiana University strives to leverage the differentiated mission of seven campuses serving undergraduate and graduate students from across Indiana, the United States, and the world. Indiana University serves over 114,000 students at its flagship research campus, an urban research campus, and five regional campuses. Campuses range in size from 4,000 students to more than 48,000 students. Improving retention and graduation rates is a top priority for the university system as outlined in the system and individual campus strategic plans. This focused commitment to student success is essential for engaging the entire university community in efforts that seek to improve student learning and achievement (Tinto & Pusser, 2006).

Of particular importance to system-wide efforts to facilitate student success are two considerations. First, each campus in the Indiana University system is unique in its structure, culture, and students. A one-size-fits-all model for any learning analytics system ignores institutional uniqueness. The systems developed at IU had to recognize differences in faculty, curricular offerings, structure, student support services, and most important, student body. Further, learning analytic systems had to accommodate a variety of uses of the data. Whereas a small, regional campus may have a centralized student success office, large campuses may approach learning analytics and associated interventions in a more distributed and decentralized fashion, with further differentiation based on factors such as student population characteristics, academic programs, and campus residence capacity.

Fostering Learning, Achievement, and Graduation Success: Implementation and Assessment of an Early Alert System

In November 2010, the IU system convened a committee to look at vended applications for an enterprise early warning system (EWS). The goal was to have an early alert system in place by fall 2011 that would support campus- and school-based efforts to improve student retention and success. Strong faculty support for an EWS was in evidence at all levels of the institution. Such a system was a key recommendation to come out of the collabora- tive regional campus strategic planning process, the *Blueprint for Student Attainment*. After extensive review of vended products, the committee de- cided that the IU system should instead build its own enterprise application. This would allow IU to promote system integration, provide as much flexi- bility for the needs of each campus and school, undertake custom program and system assessments, as well as retain ultimate control over modeling analytics. The data that would be considered for analysis fell into three cat- egories: (1) preadmission risk, (2) postadmission risk, and (3) data min- ing of past retention failures. Preadmission academic risk data included SAT/ACT scores, high school grades, quality of high school curriculum, fi- nancial resources, and parents' education. We were particularly concerned about the ethical and practical issues related to labeling students prior to their demonstrated behavior. Postadmission academic risk data included course-specific attendance and performance data, annual student survey data, learning management system activity, and so on. Data mining of re- tention failures looks at those students who failed to graduate from IU in 6 years or less (for a 4-year degree) to find attributes to identify current stu- dents for targeted intervention. Developing the system in-house meant that the data ultimately used in the system could be tailored to what made sense for each campus.

The Fostering Learning, Achievement, and Graduation Success (FLAGS) initiative consisted of multiple phases: developing an early warn- ing roster for faculty, exploring the relevance of other factors for defining risk for students before deploying that data in the system, and developing a portal for advisors (Advising Records) where this information would be aggregated and displayed and advisors could take appropriate action that could, in turn, be monitored for outcomes. The initial committee, which included diverse campus and functional area representation, continued to manage the process, beginning a new model of integrated development at IU where the eventual users of the tool stayed engaged during the design and build processes. The initiative resulted in two new tools for campus use: the Student Performance Rosters (the faculty-facing early alert option) and Advising Records (the data hub and action center). The introduction of FLAGS also created focused, sustained interest at IU in analytics and data mining to inform university practices, policies, and processes.

The Student Performance Roster (SPR) collects class-based student performance information entered by faculty in a repurposed grade roster. The tool is organized to collect four specific types of information for all students in a class: (1) attendance, (2) trends (improving, getting worse), (3) performance information (areas of faculty concern), and (4) the recom- mended action the student should take. Entering performance information requires faculty to also enter a recommended action. The SPR becomes available to faculty at the beginning of the first week of classes and remains active until final grade rosters are posted in the system. Faculty can enter data for students at any point in the semester right up until the last weeks of class.

Students can view the information (trends, performance issues, recommended actions) raised by faculty on a "My Grades" page, which advisors can also see. After much discussion, the group decided to not automatically send notification to students that they had flags. Committee members were concerned that generic messages about academic issues, especially if received more than one at a time, might lead students to disengage from the university without seeking help. Instead, each campus developed their own notification process as they saw fit. Students may be notified in the course syllabus to check their My Grades page for any flags, or an e-mail may be sent to the student about the flag from a campus registrar's office, a student retention office, or the student's academic advisor. To enable effective use and review of this tool, a series of special data dashboards—for instructors, advisors, campus administrators, and system administrators—were built in the business intelligence environment. Campuses can monitor which instructors have submitted data and can track overall submission rates and the specific performance issues and recommended actions.

Initially, many faculty saw no need to use FLAGS because they routinely reached out to students having difficulty in their classes; they did not understand that FLAGS was intended to identify students having difficulty in more than one course for better targeted support. Some faculty thought FLAGS might be useful for very large classes, where faculty–student interaction was more restricted or for freshman- and sophomore-level classes, where students were still adjusting to college expectations. Some faculty wanted to know if the students they flagged were also flagged in other courses, but IU decided not to make that information available because of concerns over negative labeling and implicit bias that would work against the students' interests.

Administrators have now begun to worry, with increased use, that faculty may stop reaching out to struggling students because they presume that because the student was flagged, support was on the way and their job was done. Many academic advisors feel they do not have enough information to work with a student who has been told "see academic advisor." Advisors have found that the student could not always articulate what the problem might be. Even with information about the behavior that triggered the flag ("irregular attendance," "missing homework," or "poor performance on quiz"), advisors often do not think they can identify the best possible intervention or treatment.

Faculty report that students often seem unaware of the flag or do not respond even if they are aware. "See instructor" was by far the most common recommended action associated with a flag, yet faculty reported that fewer than 1 in 10 students came to see them. Some faculty report that student attendance has improved even though students did not come to see them. There is significant faculty and advisor concern about ensuring that students see the alerts so that they respond to them. They want reassurance that the student has in fact read the communication or viewed the early alert. Faculty are commonly unaware whether the academic advisor knows of the alert, and they are concerned that advisors are not always following up on alerts. Some faculty want to see the communications with the flagged students and want feedback about what happened with each student they have flagged.

Several internal institutional research studies have been conducted on the effectiveness of the early alert system. One regional campus explored the relationship between when students applied for admission and what alerts were raised, finding that the earlier a student applied for admission, the less likely they were to be flagged. Another regional campus conducted several studies of early alerts and math tutoring, showing that when students seek out tutoring after being flagged, they were more likely to pass their math class. A system-wide study of the use of early alerts in the required freshman writing course produced the provocative finding that the use of FLAGS was correlated with lower average class grades. Specifically, at all but one campus, instructors who used the early alert for some of their class sections but not others had a higher percentage of poor grades (grades of D or F, or withdrawal from the class) and lower average class GPAs in the sections where alerts were used compared to the sections in which the system was not used. A study conducted at the flagship campus showed an increase in rates of course withdrawal, and an increase in the variation of grades among course completers, in courses where the early alert was used.

Vended Learning Analytics Systems: The Education Advisory Board and the Student Success Collaborative

In December 2012, central administrators announced that IU would become a founding member of the Education Advisory Board's (EAB) new Student Success Collaborative (SSC). Of the 35 institutions of higher education participating in the collaborative at that time, IU was the only multicampus member. The predictive analytics promised new insights into student behavior that could be translated into actionable interventions. This use of analytics fit well with the general direction that the university had taken with FLAGS and promised an analysis that IU had not yet developed internally, allowing internal development to focus on system redesign.

EAB developed a web-based advising platform that used 10 years of historical data on student retention, promotion, and graduation to help campuses develop "success markers" and predictive analytics for courses and majors in which each individual student was most likely to succeed. The collaborative focused on putting predictive empirical data into the hands of academic advisors in order to allow them to better determine which students needed intervention in order to graduate. In addition to course-based success markers and an overall measure of student risk, the system provided a "major-matcher" function to identify other possible majors for students who might be struggling. The system incorporated data typically stored in student information systems—course histories, term GPAs, credit accumulation, student academic standing—in graphic displays that allowed a quick check on a student's progress. Advisors could maintain dynamic work lists that tracked student progress, communicate with students as needed, and keep records of their interactions with students. Senior leadership was provided initially with broad institutional dashboards that allowed them a quick overview of the overall risk profile of their campus by school and by major within school.

In joining the collaborative, IU staff were faced with the need to integrate already ongoing work with this external framework. The SSC platform replicated some of the functions of Advising Records (note taking and student data views). Plans to expand analysis of student risk beyond the initial early alert reporting were deferred to focus on implementation of SSC. Rather than attempting to integrate the two systems, attention turned to having each campus work out clear training for advisors about why, when, and how to use each system.

Adoption of the new SSC tool into the existing suite of tools has clearly highlighted the importance of focusing on actual use in implementing any new analytics effort. IU employs a complex architecture for its student information system; advisors are able to see information for all students, regardless of their campus of enrollment. The SSC architecture required that IU's single institution feed be split out to separate campus platforms. Advisors accustomed to operating in a single institution framework were restricted to seeing only students enrolled on their campus. The separation also introduced inaccuracies into the data that advisors were quick to point out. Our first lesson was that it was critical to work with the vendor to establish a clear understanding of the input data structures; otherwise, advisors lost trust in the system and stopped using it.

The "major matcher" algorithm was too broad and did not provide actionable options. Advisors ignored success markers, a potentially useful tool for exploring risk, because the pathways and timing through degree programs on most campuses were too varied. Transfer students were flagged as at risk because they had not completed success marker courses on time; students who entered with high school dual credit were flagged as at risk because the system thought they were not accumulating credits as quickly as they should (the system looked for full-time enrollment each semester). Again, these issues led to loss in advisor trust and motivation.

Using the system revealed to us the difficulty of employing predictive analytics given the frequent changes to and evolutions of our undergraduate curriculum. General education revisions on all campuses mitigated the relevance of predictive models based on historical data. We also found that size mattered. The smaller regional campuses did not see the same predictive benefits from the analytics as the larger campuses due to a small "n" issue. Finally, the algorithm for defining risk indicators for students was not transparent; it left many advisors questioning a student's risk score. Students whom advisors knew from experience to be at high risk of completing a program were often displaying low risk levels, while students whom advisors saw as at low risk were often flagged as high risk. Our second lesson was that campus program owners had to be able to explain clearly and concisely to advisors how the platform actually worked, which was difficult when they were not privy to the algorithms.

What We Have Learned So Far

An inquiry-based approach that allowed campus stakeholders to engage in questions about the role of the campus and each student in college achievement has been of particular importance to both projects. As IU implemented these efforts, there was concern about becoming the "helicopter university," implementing support systems in such a way that students no longer needed to own their own educational process because everything was done for them. Promoting student agency and responsibility have become core values in planning for future improvements to our processes and systems.

Both systems ran into difficulty as they were implemented on our campuses, although for different reasons. The early alert system has had mixed success because there was no centralized guidance about how best to incorporate it on each campus. Without clear expectations and guidelines and a process for "closing the loop"—ensuring that students received needed support once identified—the promise of the early alert to help students succeed has been unevenly realized. The vended student success product ran into difficulties precisely because it was a one-size-fits-all model. It failed to allow us to adequately account for the internal differences of our students.

Through our collective experience, our thinking has transformed to replace the language of student "risk" with that of student "engagement." We plan to allow and promote positive as well as risk alerts, believing in the importance of skilled communication with students (that is to say, thoughtful and personalized contact, as opposed to generic information on systems pages or bulk e-mails). Our work with the SSC model—having access to specific risk data about students—helped us to rapidly change the culture of advising on all our campuses. Advisors have had good success in actively developing and carrying out proactive outreach campaigns to students. Current efforts focus on embedding this new model for advising on all our campuses. Advisors now see that serious attention is being given to the importance of advising for student success by university leadership from the president and the board of trustees, to campus leaders, to all academic and support staff. Finally, our foray into the world of predictive analytics has helped us begin discussions internally about how to support student success without becoming the "helicopter university."

Intentional and purposeful planning by our students has come to define current development priorities. These include online career education modules to embed in courses or complete through self-enrollment, an aspirational resume completed prior to orientation, and a culture of planning through our interactive Graduation Planning System. Using predictive analytics for assessing student risk demands much further research, and perhaps a semantic recasting so that it can be used to engage students based on their strengths and possibilities and not reinforce known social and economic strata.

References

Bach, C. (2010). Learning analytics: Targeting instruction, curricula and student support. *Proceedings of the Education and Information Systems, Technologies and Applications Conference*, Orlando, FL.

Bowen, E., Price, T., Lloyd, S., & Thomas, S. (2005). Improving the quantity and quality of attendance data to enhance student retention. *Journal of Further and Higher Education, 29*(4), 275–385.

Cai, Q., Lewis, C. L, & Higdon, J. (2015). Developing an early-alert system to promote student visits to tutor center. *Learning Assistance Review, 29*(2), 61–72.

Chappel, C. (2010, August 17). "Early Alert" systems send students warnings, advice. *Community College Daily.* Retrieved from http://www.ccdaily.com/Pages/Campus-Issues/Early-alert-systems-send-students-warnings-advice.aspx

Cuseo, J. (2006). Red flags: Behavioral indicators of potential student attrition. Retrieved from http://uwc.edu/sites/uwc.edu/files/imce-uploads/employees/academic-resources/esfy/_files/red_flags-behavioral_indicators_of_potential_student_attrition.pdf

Davidson, W. B., Beck, H. P., & Mulligan, M. (2009). The College Persistence Questionnaire: Development and validation of an instrument that predicts student attrition. *Journal of College Student Development, 50*(4), 373–390.

Faulconer, J., Geissler, J., Majewski, D., & Trifilo, J. (2014). Adoption of an early-alert system to support university student success. *Delta Kappa Gamma Bulletin, 80*(2), 45–48.

Hudson, W. E. (2005). Can an early alert excessive absenteeism warning system be effective in retaining freshman students? *Journal of College Student Retention: Research, Theory & Practice, 7*(3), 217–226.

Lonn, S., Krumm, A. E., Waddington, R. J., & Teasley, S. D. (2012). Bridging the gap from knowledge to action: Putting analytics in the hands of academic advisors. *LAK '12 Proceedings of the 2nd International Conference on Learning Analytics and Knowledge.* New York, NY: ACM. https://doi.org/10.1145/2330601.2330647

Pistilli, M. D., & Arnold, K. E. (2010). Purdue Signals: Mining real-time academic data to enhance student success. *About Campus, 15*(3), 22–24.

Simmons, J. M. (2011). A national study of student early alert models at four-year institutions of higher education (Doctoral dissertation). Retrieved from ProQuest Dissertations and Theses database. (UMI 3482551).

Tampke, D. R. (2013). Developing, implementing, and assessing an early alert system. *Journal of College Student Retention: Research, Theory & Practice, 14*(4), 523–532.

Tinto, V., & Pusser, B. (2006). *Moving from theory to action: Building a model of institutional action for student success*. Report commissioned by the National Postsecondary Education Cooperative. Washington, DC: U.S. Department of Education.

Wagner, E., & Ice, P. (2012). Data changes everything: Delivering on the promise of learning analytics in higher education. *EDUCAUSE Review, 47*(4), 32–42.

Wagner, E., & Longanecker, D. (2016). Scaling student success with predictive analytics: Reflections after four years in the data trenches. *Change, 48*(1), 52–58.

CATHERINE BUYARSKI *is an Associate Dean for Student Affairs and Executive Director for Student Success Initiatives for University College at IUPUI.*

JIM MURRAY *is the Manager of the Academic Advising Enterprise Student Systems group at Indiana University.*

REBECCA TORSTRICK *is a Professor of Anthropology and Assistant Vice President for University Academic Affairs and Director of the Office of Completion and Student Success at Indiana University.*

NEW DIRECTIONS FOR HIGHER EDUCATION • DOI: 10.1002/he

The implementation of analytics in support of student success requires effective use of feedback and interventions, as well as a system by which the use of feedback and institutional supports can be tracked and evaluated.

Learner Analytics and Student Success Interventions

Matthew D. Pistilli

Imagine this scenario: You are a new faculty member and have been assigned to teach three sections of an introductory psychology class. When you receive your course rosters, you realize that over 200 students will be in each section, that you know nothing about these students, and that the department chair has charged you with increasing success rates in the course. As the first assignments and assessments of the semester come around, you notice that you have a wide range of performance, including a large proportion of students earning a C or less. Given that you teach over 600 students and have other requirements as a faculty member, you wonder how you might be able to provide meaningful feedback to students in a data-driven and efficient manner.

Enter learner analytics. Learner analytics is a more focused realm of the more widely known learning analytics. Defined by the Society of Learning Analytics Research (SoLAR, 2012), learning analytics focuses on "the measurement, collection, analysis and reporting of data about learners and their contexts, for purposes of understanding and optimizing learning and the environments in which it occurs." This is a prime example of institutions turning to business intelligence techniques that utilize prescriptive interventions to augment and support student success.

While learning can be optimized at the course or section level, learner analytics looks for the variables contributing to risks faced by individual learners, and helps to identify targeted interventions that mitigate the risks individual learners experience while participating in their academic work. The end state of learner analytics is to identify risk and determine which interventions are likely to get the right prescriptive information to the right learners at the right time in the right way so that their performance improves.

NEW DIRECTIONS FOR HIGHER EDUCATION, no. 179, Fall 2017 © 2017 Wiley Periodicals, Inc.
Published online in Wiley Online Library (wileyonlinelibrary.com) • DOI: 10.1002/he.20242

The Right Information to the Right Students

The first component of intervening with students is to determine what information needs to be presented to students. Here, we must begin with intent. What message needs to be conveyed to students? Do they need to know the grade they have earned on an assignment? Do they need to know they're not performing at a level that will ensure success in the course? Does the instructor simply want to communicate the fact that resources exist to help students be successful, regardless of current performance? Ultimately, in order to present the right information—indeed, a relative term depending on perspective—one must first determine what needs to be provided. That will shape both the message crafted and the delivery mechanism employed.

The Roles of Feedback in Advising and Academic Achievement

Feedback is an exchange between two or more persons—which can be done in person or mediated by a computer or phone—so that individuals are better informed about the extent to which their work was done correctly or incorrectly, or where they are with relation to specific course outcomes (Tanes, Arnold, Selzer King, & Remnet, 2011). Chickering and Gamson (1987) note that frequent feedback is best—"students need chances to reflect on what they have learned, what they still need to know, and how to assess themselves" (p. 5). Tunstall and Gipps (1996) take this further, indicating that the use of feedback can bring to light what students have learned and what they are able to do as a result. Ultimately, Hattie and Timperley (2007) describe feedback as "one of the most powerful influences on learning and achievement" (p. 81).

Feedback brings with it many positive outcomes. In higher education environments, greater levels of interaction between students and faculty can lead to cognitive and personal development for students (Astin, 1993). Feedback students perceive as being fair or encouraging is seen as more effective (Lizzio & Wilson, 2008) and is even more effective when the person providing the feedback is viewed as being highly credible (Poulos & Mahony, 2008). When feedback is issued to students from credible sources, is fair or encouraging, and is provided in a timely manner, students are more likely to learn from experiences in ways that should make them more successful in the future. By inserting learning theory into the implementation of analytics, institutions can ensure a strong implementation and the greatest chance of realizing successful outcomes.

Social Cognitive Theory

Learning from experiences is at the core of Bandura's (1977) social cognitive theory (SCT), and feedback is a key way to inform students about actions that can be taken to improve a course outcome. SCT tells us that learning occurs in situations where people can engage with tasks or problems as well as through observing those around them work on similar endeavors. Students are motivated by a specific outcome perceived to be desirable—or at least more desirable than their current situation, something instructors can provide through a learning analytics–driven intervention. Bandura (2001) also notes that by reviewing expectations, people aim to achieve outcomes that are positive in nature. Put differently, students examine the potential consequences associated with various courses of action and plan their next steps accordingly. This agentic approach, where students are able to "exercise some control over" (Bandura, 1991, p. 249) the ways in which they plan to deal with a situation, solve a problem, feel about something, or become motivated to act at all, is the basis for a person's self-efficacy (Bandura, 1986).

Self-efficacy is rooted in a person's self-appraisal of the beliefs they hold about their abilities to perform various actions or tasks (Bandura, 1977, 1986). Applying self-efficacy to the educational environment, Schunk (1990) describes students' perception of their ability to apply the necessary behaviors or knowledge within a classroom. Studies, such as those conducted by Zajacova, Lynch, and Espenshade (2005) and Gore (2006), demonstrate that academic self-efficacy both strongly predicts first-year college student success and grows over the course of a semester as students experience success. Student success influenced by feedback sets a "psychological stage for a successful college experience" (Betz, 2007, p. 409).

Part of that stage setting involves timing information presented to students so that it can be as effective as possible. It is also important to consider the messages and the media employed to garner the greatest effect. Torrance (2012) illustrates this need, noting that feedback cannot be something that is just given to students, but is actually something that can be "acted upon" (p. 330). Torrance also points that there is an emotional toll associated with receiving feedback that affects how students feel about themselves and their abilities. It is important that the information provided to students be formative in nature—both in the intent behind the feedback (to help students improve) and in the effect portrayed (so that students do not feel defeated). While feedback to students is not always positive, it can be provided in ways that promote learning and growth. However, simply providing feedback is insufficient; we must also look to inform the learning process for both students and instructors.

The Right Time in the Right Way

Not all feedback is created equally, and the delivery of feedback in and of itself is rarely sufficient with regard to helping a student succeed. Learning analytics provides an opportunity to better inform both learners and teachers and the ways in which feedback can be derived from a learning analytics solution and presented to students varies greatly.

Analytics-driven feedback must connect information provided to students to context in both relevant and timely manners. Feedback, applied appropriately, can also help to influence effective learning dispositions (Gray, McGuinness, Owende, & Hofmann, 2016), including deep learning approaches, students being able to self-regulate themselves around getting coursework done, setting learning goals, and increasing intellectual curiosity.

Khan and Pardo (2016) examined feedback effectiveness via the ways in which students employed dashboards showing course performance over time. They found no correlation between the use of the dashboard, which reflected course performance, and students' grades; however, they did find that students did, in fact, want to have feedback presented to them. In the narrative of not all feedback being created equal, this is an example of how simply telling students how they were doing was ineffective; more qualitative feedback was determined to be necessary in order to help students improve their performance over time.

In Chapter 6 of this volume, Fritz describes the effect of providing feedback to students on the number of times they were logging into the learning management system (LMS) as compared to their peers, what their grade was, and what were the general grades of those who had more or less interaction with the LMS than themselves. While the Check My Activity feedback is still dashboard based, the ability of students to drill into the information presented to them, and subsequently use that information to change their study habits and behaviors, resulted in students using the system to be nearly twice as likely to get at least a C in a course when compared to those who had access to Check My Activity but never used it.

The desire for feedback should not be surprising. Most students go to college to learn, and they expect to be guided in that endeavor. The challenge, then, is not knowing *if* students want feedback, but, rather, in *how* to provide it to them in ways that will be effective. Gettings, Waters, Selzer King, Tanes, and Pistilli (2013) and Ehle and Gettings (2013) conducted studies at Purdue University to get directly at this.

At Purdue, faculty had access to a system called *Course Signals*, a technology developed by Instructional Technology at Purdue and later licensed to Ellucian. Course Signals is a learning analytics technology

developed on a predictive analytic model that contains elements from the academic technologies and the student information system. The model is behaviorally based and considers student performance, effort, and characteristics. The algorithm runs on real-time data and provides a risk indicator for each student. Using this risk indicator (a red, yellow, or green traffic signal) as a formative guide, faculty members can give students in their courses meaningful feedback, suggesting behaviors that students might wish to change to improve their chances of success, thus placing the emphasis squarely on action. (Pistilli, Arnold, & Bethune, 2012, para 5)

Gettings et al.'s (2013) study focused on what students wanted to get for feedback via e-mail from instructors using Course Signals in their classes. Students in the study first provided reactions to messages they might receive from an instructor about their course performance. Afterwards, they were asked to rewrite the messages presented to them in ways that would be more palatable to them, composing messages for students performing poorly in a course, students doing moderately well, and students showing no signs of struggle. Student-written messages were examined for positive and negative effect, self-efficacy promotion, perceived motivational effects, and the extent to which a message facilitated interaction with the instructor.

Several key findings emerged from the examination of students' responses to the instruments and the messages they wrote that all correspond to general theories of feedback. First, and as discussed by Chickering and Gamson (1987), Hartley and Chesworth (2000), Thompson and Mazer (2009), and Yorke and Longden (2006), among others, the concept of "early and often" feedback is paramount. Prompt feedback is important—providing feedback about performance on homework after a test on the same concept has been taken is wholly ineffective. Feedback must be presented in a timely enough manner so that students can take it into account as they move forward.

Furthermore, providing the same feedback in multiple formats, such as e-mail, broad course discussions, and one-on-one conversations, was also seen as highly beneficial for the students. Gettings et al. (2013) also found that including dates or references to recent campus or class events (for example, a test, homecoming, or spring break) lent both relevancy and credibility to messages. Wise's (2014) research also indicates that the timeliness and relevance of feedback is essential in order for appropriate meaning to be made by the learner.

Students indicated that they wanted *explicit* feedback; that is, they wanted direct actions they could take to maintain or improve their grades or performance, which concurs with Tanes et al.'s (2011) finding that feedback emphasizing outcomes, rather than past behaviors, would be the most successful. Gettings et al. (2013) also noted that students desired feedback that focused on the outcomes of specific behaviors. Telling students to simply spend more time studying was found to be ineffective, while indicating that students who spend a certain amount of time studying a specific topic in a given manner (such as flash cards for anatomy or group studying for biology labs) tended to do better overall and feedback was received much more openly and readily by students.

Ultimately, however, not all students respond the same way to similar kinds of feedback. Smith, Lange, and Huston (2012) found that among online community college students, those receiving direct contact via phone or voicemail fared much better than those to whom outreach efforts were unsuccessful (wrong or disconnected numbers, no answer). Separately, e-mails automatically sent to students at the beginning of a term suggesting that students log in to their courses on the first day of the course resulted in a 40% decrease in students dropping the course later in the term for some groups of students, but not for all classes tested.

The construction of messages, along with their tone, also play a role in their effectiveness. Messages perceived to be encouraging of progress, regardless of actual performance, yielded increased levels of self-efficacy, which in turn facilitated student success. Messages threatening students were wholly ineffective. Furthermore, messages that were interpreted as constructive in nature and encouraging in tone were determined to be the most effective of all. These results are bolstered by research conducted by Bjorklund, Parente, and Sathianathan (2004) and Lizzio and Wilson (2008), who found that constructive and encouraging feedback is more effective and increases students' gains in problem solving and communication skills.

A separate study conducted by Wise, Zhao, and Hausknecht (2013) noted that analysis of interventions resulted not only in online students recognizing utility in the information presented to them but also that students quickly noticed that information was not included in the algorithm that prompted the intervention to be initiated. Aguilar, Lonn, and Teasley (2014) note that interviews with students can help to mitigate this disconnect, as well as shape appropriate interventions and messaging to students. Additionally, Aguilar et al. (2014) indicated the importance of also seeking feedback from those actually doing the intervening, be that faculty, staff, or peers, regardless of method.

Ultimately, simply providing feedback for the sake of feedback is unnecessary; there must be intentionality behind the feedback, and those intentions need to consider how the information will be received and what students can do with it.

Too Much of a Good Thing?

Feedback, while important to student performance, personal development, and academic self-efficacy, can also create challenges for students. Tanes et al. (2011) noted that lengthy feedback is generally unsuccessful. While students in danger of doing poorly in a class need more information on how to improve their performance, there is a risk of giving too much detail to students such that they won't read the messages at all. As Tanes et al. (2011) state, "instructors should succinctly focus on ways to improve student outcomes" in their feedback to students (p. 2420).

Beyond the message length itself, there is also the possibility that too much feedback in general can have deleterious effects. Wise (2014) cautions that the overuse of feedback derived from analytics, what she terms "omnipresent analytics," presents two specific dangers. First, the notion of receiving feedback at any time or in any place can result in the feedback never being reviewed. Basically, too much information received too often is ineffective. Second, Wise indicates that the constant attention to numbers or metrics can find students playing to the numbers in an effort to get the best possible score but not engaging with the material in an effort to learn it.

In short, there is an optimal window of how much information to provide to students, how often to provide it, and the tone to strike in the feedback itself. To determine what the appropriate window, manner, and tone is, one must talk to both the provider and the receiver of feedback.

Closing the Loop: Considerations for Implementation

The prospect of providing feedback to students is only effective if the extent to which that feedback was helpful is determined. Barring some form of assessment, it is impossible to know if any messaging or interventions provided were actually effective. Clow (2012) notes that it also is important to examine intermediate efforts, like interventions, and not just look to assess the outcome of our actions.

As such, developing interventions and administering them as part of an analytics endeavor requires careful thought and planning. This thought should include input from many different levels of stakeholders. Drachsler and Greller (2012) discuss stakeholders in the realm of those who are "the contributors and beneficiaries of learning analytics ... [including] *data clients* as well as *data subjects*" (p. 120, emphasis in original). Data clients usually are those who benefit from the data and who will be doing the acting upon the results of the analytic algorithm. One might conceptualize the data clients as teachers or administrators of various academic resources. Data subjects, on the other hand, are usually those whose data is supplied to the algorithm or process, or, most often, the students being affected by this implementation.

So often analytics are viewed as a way of identifying students at risk of something, be that failing a course, leaving an institution, or engaging in some other behavior. To the contrary, analytics must drive faculty–student interaction, which Draschler and Greller (2012) note is one of the greatest potential benefits of implementing learning analytics. Nelson Laird, Chen, and Kuh's (2008) and Chickering and Gamson's (1987) research underscores this, demonstrating that institutions that have higher-than-normal levels of student success have increased levels of faculty–student interaction. However, the outcomes of any learner analytics effort must be measured. Analysis of the kinds of interventions provided, language or methodologies employed, and their overall effectiveness must be fully assessed— and done so in ways that identify diagnostic, predictive, and prescriptive methods that support educational transformation efforts (Casonato, Lapkin, Beyer, Genovese, & Friedman, 2011).

Transforming higher education may seem like an impossible daunting task. However, learner analytics can take this seemingly impossible task and make it much more manageable through creating a means to provide meaningful, targeted feedback to identified students in efficient and effective manners. Through providing feedback to students, and examining the rhetoric employed and effect portrayed therein, we create a highly powerful means of helping students not only improve their performance but also become better overall students.

References

Aguilar, S., Lonn, S., & Teasley, S. D. (2014). Perceptions and use of an early warning system during a higher education transition program. In K. Arnold, S. Teasley, & A. Pardo (Eds.), *Proceedings from the Fourth International Conference on Learning Analytics and Knowledge* (pp. 113–117), New York, NY: ACM. https://doi.org/10.1145/2567574. 2567625

Astin, A. W. (1993). What matters in college? *Liberal Education, 79*(4), 4–16.

Bandura, A. (1977). Self-efficacy: Toward a unifying theory of behavior change. *Psychological Review, 84*(2), 191–215.

Bandura, A. (1986). Social foundations of thought and action: A social cognitive theory. Englewood Cliffs, NJ: Prentice-Hall.

Bandura, A. (1991). Social cognitive theory of self-regulation. *Organizational Behavior and Human Decision Processes, 50*(2), 248–287.

Bandura, A. (2001). Social cognitive theory: An agentic perspective. *Annual Review of Psychology, 52*(1), 1–26.

Betz, N. E. (2007). Career self-efficacy: Exemplary recent research and emerging directions. *Journal of Career Assessment, 15*(4), 403–422.

Bjorklund, S. A., Parente, J. M., & Sathianathan, D. (2004). Effects of faculty interaction and feedback on gains in student skills. *Journal of Engineering Education, 93*(2), 153–160.

Casonato, R., Lapkin, A., Beyer, M. A., Genovese, Y., & Friedman, T. (2011). Information management in the 21st century. Stamford, CT: Gartner. Retrieved from https://www.gartner.com/doc/1781917/information-management-st-century

Chickering, A. W., & Gamson, Z. F. (1987). Seven principles for good practice in undergraduate education. *AAHE Bulletin, 39*(7), 3–7.

Clow, D. (2012). The learning analytics cycle: Closing the loop. In D. Gašević & S. Buckingham Shum (Eds.), *Proceedings from the 2nd International Learning Analytics & Knowledge Conference*, pp. 134–138. New York: ACM. https://doi.org/10.1145/. 23306012330636

Drachsler, H., & Greller, W. (2012). The pulse of learning analytics: Understandings and expectations from the stakeholders. In D. Gašević & S. Buckingham Shum (Eds.), *Proceedings from the 2nd International Learning Analytics & Knowledge Conference*, pp. 120–129. New York, NY: ACM. https://doi.org/10.1145/2330601.2330634

Ehle, Z. T., & Gettings, P. (2013). *The role of computer mediated instructional message quality on perceived message effects in an academic analytics intervention*. Paper presented at International Communications Association Annual Conference, London, UK.

Gettings, P. E., Waters, J., Selzer King, A., Tanes, Z., & Pistilli, M. D. (2013). Message testing and self-efficacy in Course Signals: Formative evaluation to identify effective communication strategies. Paper presented at the Southern States Communication Association Annual Conference, Louisville, KY.

Gore, P. A., Jr. (2006). Academic self-efficacy as a predictor of college outcomes. *Journal of Career Assessment, 14*(1), 92–115.

Gray, G., McGuinness, C., Owende, P., & Hofmann, M. (2016). Learning factor models of students at risk of failing in the early stage of tertiary education. *Journal of Learning Analytics, 3*(2), 330–372.

Hartley, J., & Chesworth, K. (2000). Qualitative and quantitative methods in research on essay writing: No one way. *Journal of Further and Higher Education, 24*(1), 15–24.

Hattie, J., & Timperley, H. (2007). The power of feedback. *Review of Higher Education, 77*(1), 81–122.

Khan, I., & Pardo, A. (2016). Data2U: Scalable real-time student feedback in active learning environments. In S. Dawson, H. Drachsler, & C. P. Rosé (Eds.), *Proceedings from the 6th International Conference on Learning Analytics and Knowledge* (pp. 249–253), New York, NY: ACM. https://doi.org/10.1145/2883851.2883911

Lizzio, A., & Wilson, K. (2008). Feedback on assessment: Students' perceptions of quality and effectiveness. *Assessment & Evaluation in Higher Education, 33*(3), 263–275.

Nelson Laird, T. F., Chen, D., & Kuh, G. D. (2008). Classroom practices at institutions with higher-than-expected persistence rates: What student engagement data tell us. In J. Braxton (Ed.), *New Directions for Teaching and Learning* (no. 115), pp. 85–99, San Francisco: Jossey-Bass.

Pistilli, M. D., Arnold, K., & Bethune, M. (2012). Signals: Using academic analytics to promote student success. *EDUCAUSE Review Online*. Retrieved from http://www.educause.edu/ero/article/signals-using-academic-analytics-promote-student-success

Poulos, A., & Mahony, M. J. (2008). Effectiveness of feedback: The students' perspective. *Assessment & Evaluation in Higher Education, 33*(2), 143–154.

Schunk, D. H. (1990). Goal setting and self-efficacy during self-regulated learning. *Educational Psychologist, 25*(1), 71–86.

Smith, V. C., Lange, A., & Huston, D. R. (2012). Predictive modeling to forecast student outcomes and drive effective interventions in online community college courses. *Journal of Asynchronous Learning Networks, 16*(3), 51–61.

SoLAR (Society for Learning Analytics Research). (2012). About. Retrieved from http://www.solaresearch.org/about/

Tanes, Z., Arnold, K., Selzer King, A., & Remnet, M. A. (2011). Using Signals for appropriate feedback: Perceptions and practices. *Computers & Education, 57*, 2414–2422.

Thompson, B., & Mazer, J. P. (2009). College student ratings of student academic support: Frequency, importance, and modes of communication. *Communication Education, 58*(3), 433–458.

Torrance, H. (2012). Formative assessment at the crossroads: Conformative, deformative and transformative assessment. *Oxford Review of Education, 38*(3), 323–342.

Tunstall, P., & Gipps, C. (1996). Teacher feedback to young children in formative assessment: A typology. *British Educational Research Journal, 22*(4), 389–404.

Wise, A. F. (2014). Designing pedagogical interventions to support student use of learning analytics. In S. Teasley & A. Pardo (Eds.), *Proceedings of the 4th International Conference on Learning Analytics and Knowledge* (pp. 203–211). New York, NY: ACM. https://doi.org/10.1145/2567574.2567588

Wise, A. F., Zhao, Y., & Hausknecht, S. N. (2013). Learning analytics for online discussions: A pedagogical model for intervention with embedded and extracted analytics. In D. Suthers, K. Verbert, E. Duval, & X. Ochoa (Eds.), *Proceedings of the Third International Conference on Learning Analytics and Knowledge* (pp. 46–48), New York, NY: ACM. https://doi.org/10.1145/2460296.2460308

Yorke, M., & Longden, B. (2006). The vital first year. *Academy Exchange, 4*, 16–17.

Zajacova, A., Lynch, S. M., & Espenshade, T. J. (2005). Self-efficacy, stress, and academic success in college. *Research in Higher Education, 46*(6), 677–706.

DR. MATTHEW D. PISTILLI *is the Director of Student Affairs Assessment & Research for the Division of Student Affairs at Iowa State University.*

5

This chapter details the process the University of Michigan developed to build institutional capacity for learning analytics. A symposium series, faculty task force, fellows program, research grants, and other initiatives are discussed, with lessons learned for future efforts and how other institutions might adapt such efforts to spur cultural change to utilize institutional data to improve teaching and learning processes.

Cultivating Institutional Capacities for Learning Analytics

Steven Lonn, Timothy A. McKay, Stephanie D. Teasley

As the 21st century neared, many large U.S. postsecondary institutions began to reevaluate their long-held practices of maintaining student records. Computerized systems became the norm; institutions began developing electronic student information systems (SISs) to record and store student records. However, many institutions failed to realize the potential for research on teaching and learning outcomes that lay within SISs and other enterprise technology systems. At the University of Michigan (U-M), there was some early interest in this data by designing a basic query tool for faculty to visualize simple frequencies and correlations (Academic Reporting Toolkit, circa 2002), but the data mainly languished in separate and unintegrated, institutional databases for each functional area (admissions, registration, human resources, research, and so on).

Two early efforts at U-M laid the groundwork for the later analytics community. First, inspired from the work by Freeman and colleagues (2007) that predicted student performance in introductory biology using GPA and SAT scores, three physics faculty members investigated student performance in physics courses, identified those who did better and worse than predicted and investigated potential reasons why (Wright, McKay, Hershock, Miller, & Tritz, 2014). Second, the USE Lab, an interdisciplinary research lab investigating the intersection of learning technologies in higher education teaching led by Stephanie Teasley, a research professor in the School of Information, conducted a series of studies investigating perceptions and aggregated use of the institutional learning management system (for example, Lonn & Teasley, 2009).

New Directions for Higher Education, no. 179, Fall 2017 © 2017 Wiley Periodicals, Inc.
Published online in Wiley Online Library (wileyonlinelibrary.com) • DOI: 10.1002/he.20243

While these early efforts at U-M were primarily faculty-led, a variety of academic and support staff as well as students of all levels need to be involved in creating a culture of awareness and acceptance for learning analytics (Arnold, Lonn, & Pistilli, 2014). Cultivating institutional capacities from these members of the university community can, and should, include a variety of opportunities, at multiple levels of engagement, in order to elicit the broadest possible support from the institutional community of scholars, researchers, and professionals. While not the only blueprint for such cultural development, the authors of this chapter detail the various components of the efforts undertaken at the University of Michigan from 2011 to 2015 so other institutions may reflect on the lessons learned and adopt or adapt similar efforts to their own institutional contexts.

The Origin of the Symposium on Learning Analytics at Michigan and the Learning Analytics Community

The University of Michigan, like many large U.S. higher education institutions with very high research activity, is highly decentralized. Interactions among faculty members, particularly across disciplinary lines, are often haphazard and unplanned. This was the case for the two faculty members at the epicenter of the launch of the learning analytics community at U-M in early 2011. Timothy McKay, an Arthur F. Thurnau Professor of Physics and Astronomy, had recently been awarded a Next Generation Learning Challenge (NGLC) Grant from the Bill & Melinda Gates Foundation to launch ECoach, a tailored message tool to guide students through physics classes using analytics-powered algorithms and personalized testimonials. Meanwhile, Teasley's USE Lab had recently launched Student Explorer, an early warning system that gathered data from the institutional learning management system and delivered categorized warning signals to students' academic advisors, who could then interpret and act upon the simplified data presentation.

These professors, and their projects, were introduced via a mutual colleague (thanks to Ann Verhey-Henke) as word of McKay's NGLC grant spread among faculty involved in technology initiatives at U-M. Seeing an opportunity to not only share insights among known colleagues but also build a community around the nascent field of academic and learning analytics, McKay and Teasley submitted a proposal to U-M's Rackham Graduate School and Office of the Vice-President for Research to launch an interdisciplinary seminar series (McKay & Teasley, 2011). The proposal highlighted the promise of bringing new techniques to bear on student data:

> Mining available data and using academic analytics can provide a rich portrait of each student's progress through the university; a map of their journey from application, through the curriculum, to graduation. Performance at every stage is recorded, at a minimum as course grades, but often in more

detailed ways. … This information can tell us a tremendous amount about how students progress from naïve beginners to graduates, how they navigate the university, and how they learn.

The proposal also highlighted the fact that the necessary expertise about learning theory, student success, data mining, visualization, and predictive modeling is diffused across many domains at an institution like U-M. The central idea was to bring together students, faculty, and staff interested in analytics in a compelling series of seminars that would spur future collaborations and research projects.

This symposium proposal was accepted and planning began in earnest to line up internal and external speakers. McKay and Steven Lonn, a postdoctoral scholar in Teasley's research lab, assumed much of the planning responsibilities, focusing mainly on educational research projects across multiple disciplines that could be considered early learning analytics projects. Lonn suggested the acronym SLAM for the "Symposium on Learning Analytics at Michigan."

SLAM launched on September 14, 2011, with several dozen U-M faculty, students, and staff in attendance to hear McKay discuss this new series and his own work investigating years of physics students at U-M (Miller, 2011). This led to the creation of the ECoach project. U-M chemistry researchers and the director of U-M's writing center followed in subsequent SLAM sessions. External speakers John Campbell from Purdue University and David Pritchard from the Massachusetts Institute of Technology rounded out the first five sessions of SLAM.

Lonn recorded all of the first-year SLAM talks and slides on an institutional website to serve as an archive and learning materials for the U-M community. In all, 14 internal and three external speakers or teams presented in the first year of SLAM—all of whose presentations and materials are available today as a nationally visible resource (Center for Research on Learning and Teaching, 2017). As the learning analytics community at U-M grew, this historical record was valuable to understand the context and growing institutional knowledge in this emergent field.

Establishing a Learning Analytics Task Force

With the aim of growing and supporting a larger learning analytics research community at U-M, McKay reached out to campus leadership to provide funding and a process to foster early learning analytics-related investigations. As Cameron (1984) writes, higher education institutions often respond to complexity in their environment by producing new complex local structures for task management. Learning analytics, specifically, requires leadership to navigate significant and strategic changes to organizational culture and behavior (Baepler & Murdoch, 2010; Norris, Baer, & Offerman, 2009). McKay, a longtime faculty member at U-M and an established leader in a variety of administrative committees, was therefore a perfect fit to champion the launch of learning analytics efforts at a large and diverse research university like U-M.

After the first successful semester of the SLAM series, McKay met with the university provost, Philip Hanlon, to discuss support for learning analytics at U-M. McKay had served on the faculty governance's Academic Affairs Advisory Committee that had recently completed an internal assessment report that highlighted the various ways data was used at the institution, particularly in the area of increasing methodologies and techniques to analyze large amounts of student data. Hanlon committed $2 million of internal funds to support learning analytics through the establishment of a 3-year faculty governance body: the Learning Analytics Task Force (LATF) (McKay, 2012).

Chaired by McKay, the LATF membership comprised 12 faculty members from a cross-section of disciplines—an early attempt to reflect the cross-disciplinary interest in learning analytics. The LATF was charged with "designing a program of activities to draw out, support, and execute the best ideas in learning analytics at Michigan." Three primary goals were included in this charge: (1) explore the U-M information environment and recommend to the Provost improvements to make U-M a world-class environment for learning analytics research, (2) design and execute a funding program to support the best learning analytics projects proposed by the university community, and (3) review the metrics used to assess teaching and learning at U-M.

In support of these goals, the LATF supported several major activities. First, the SLAM seminars would continue under the auspices of the U-M Center for Research on Learning and Teaching. Between 2012 and 2015, 37 different presentations were offered from internal and external speakers and teams. Nearly 2,000 attendees representing nearly every school and college at U-M engaged with the presenters in real time, and all of the presentations were recorded and materials provided online. These videos, on topics such as improving peer education through analytics and using learning analytics in pedagogical design, have received over 8,500 total views worldwide. The 4 years of SLAM were instrumental in providing a space for learning, sharing insights, and engaging with leading researchers—it is doubtful that the learning analytics community today at U-M would be as disciplinarily diverse without the SLAM series as an initial catalyst.

University of Michigan–Funded Learning Analytics Grants

In support of its charge to design and execute a funding program to support analytics projects, the LATF created two programs to facilitate the growing learning analytics research community at U-M. For researchers and teams who were ready to launch a significant research project, the Exploring Learning Analytics (ELA) grant program provided both financial (up to $150,000) and technical support. ELA grants were designed to support the analysis of data generated in academic activities at U-M with the goal of better understanding teaching and learning on campus, and to contribute intellectually to the U-M learning analytics community.

ELA grant proposals were evaluated on a quarterly basis during the first year and a half of the LATF tenure, allowing time for funded proposals to report on initial findings. Proposals were evaluated on several criteria including the potential impact on the student experience, the potential to expand and improve the use of learning analytics, the appropriateness of the project team to meet its stated goals, and the contribution to the interdisciplinary mix of ELA projects. In all, 16 proposals were received, resulting in eight funded ELA projects:

1. Engaging Faculty with Learning Analytics: Developing New Tools to Support Departmental Assessment
2. Customized Course Advising at Michigan
3. Engaged Advising: Using Data to Construct a Narrative for Success
4. Expanding E2Coach to Enhance Student Success in Introductory STEM Courses
5. Library Analytics for Student Success
6. Arts at Michigan: Arts Engagement Project
7. Using LA to Coach Students to "Electrifying" Careers
8. Playful Analytics: Infusing a Learning Management System with Analytics that Motivate Learning and Support Teaching

The results of these eight projects varied from uncovering previously unknown facts and trends about student learning and performance to new tools and techniques for analyzing data. For example, the "Customized Course Advising" project revealed that engineering freshmen who received a 4 on their Math AB Advanced Placement exam only received an A or B grade 50% of the time when enrolling in Calculus II their first term (Nam, Lonn, Brown, Davis, & Koch, 2014). This finding resulted in academic advisors' critical analysis of students' math placement exam scores before recommending an initial math course to students. Several ELA projects investigated the use and outcomes of developing analytics-powered tools including ECoach, Student Explorer, and GradeCraft, a new learning management system for gameful course environments. In all, the ELA projects were instrumental in advancing the analysis and tools of learning analytics research at U-M, particularly when paired with the LATF's other funding program: the learning analytics fellows.

The Learning Analytics Fellows Program

Recognizing that growing a learning analytics research community included not only providing funds for projects but also providing a learning environment in which to foster the development of learning analytics skills and knowledge, the LATF launched the learning analytics fellows program in January 2013. The call for applications was released in November 2012 for both junior (graduate students and postdoctoral scholars) and senior (faculty and staff) fellows. Fellows were required to meet weekly throughout the winter semester; discuss methodological, ethical, policy, and pedagogical issues and implications of analytics research; attend SLAM seminars; and work on small-scale research projects to develop research plans. Each junior fellow received $2,000 and each senior fellow received $4,000 cash stipends to support their analytics efforts (for example, paying for temporary student help, professional development, and so on).

The winter 2013 cohort of learning analytics fellows consisted of 15 junior fellows and 16 senior fellows. The syllabus for this initial cohort included an introduction to institutional data sets, course recommender systems, data visualization, course-level data, noncognitive factors, the institutional review board (IRB) and the Family Educational Rights and Privacy Act (FERPA), and data ethics and privacy. Many of the fellows in this initial class used the funds to support their initial research ideas or later submitted proposals for ELA grants and other national grants. For example, three of the fellows from the Chemistry Department (Shultz, Winschel, & Gottfried, 2015) analyzed the impact of a general chemistry prerequisite on later student achievement and progression in subsequent chemistry courses.

The winter 2014 cohort of learning analytics fellows was deliberately smaller (19 fellows). The call for fellows explicitly solicited teams of junior and senior members who specified a nascent project idea that they would like to explore during the semester. The syllabus in the second cohort also reflected the growing breadth and varied interests of the community—the topics included natural language processing, prediction models, dashboards, learning measurements, stereotype threat, and behavioral change. Again, the projects developed during the cohort led to several grant proposals and scholarly papers (for example, Brooks, Chavez, Tritz, & Teasley, 2015).

On March 27, 2015, McKay reflected on the lasting impact of the fellows program:

> ...many projects were done by the fellows, and they discovered a bunch of important *things*—and that helped us to better understand what the space was that's out there.

> This *idea*—that if you give people the data and you give them the opportunity to explore, *great things will happen*—is the reason for having the most open possible datasets that we can. And it's one of the things we have to remember as an institution as we think about the concerns we might have when opening data. You know there's always some risk in letting people go look at data. But

there's also a lot of benefit that comes from it. And we have to make sure that we continue to articulate that benefit at the same time people get nervous about risks.

The learning analytics fellows program also had several tangible results that helped streamline the process to connect U-M researchers to the appropriate institutional data to answer their learning analytics questions. First, the IRB became much more attuned to the nature and types of research questions that are typical in learning analytics research, and thus better able to direct researchers to appropriate approval processes for those projects that could typically be considered exempt from ongoing IRB review and those that needed to follow the nonexempt review process. Second, the Office of General Council developed a streamlined memorandum of understanding document for the fellows program that defined how the fellows were to comply with FERPA and data security standards. Finally, Lonn, recognizing a demonstrated need for more normalized institutional data for learning analytics research, began to work with analytics researchers and institutional technology staff members to develop and maintain a new learning analytics data architecture dataset to support the next generation of learning analytics research initiatives (see https://enrollment.umich.edu/data-research/learning-analytics-data-architecture-larc).

New Metrics, Cross-Institutional Research, and Analytics-Driven Cultural Change

The third charge of the LATF was to review the metrics used to assess teaching and learning at U-M. To that end, a subcommittee of the LATF investigated the core teaching evaluation questions filled out by students at the end of every course. This project found that evaluations were fairly consistent and were significantly correlated with evaluations posted on the Rate-MyProfessors website. One significant outcome from this project was the recognition that the existing university-wide standard questions did not reflect the types of teaching and learning outcomes that the faculty sought to recognize. After a report to the faculty governance body and significant deliberation, a new set of eight evaluation questions (four old, four new) were developed and established as of fall term 2016 to better reflect a variety of dimensions about each learning environment.

After the first year of the SLAM seminars, McKay presented the concept of the LATF and the learning analytics efforts at U-M to a meeting of all of the provosts in the Big Ten Academic Alliance. The provosts endorsed an effort to compare learning analytics metrics and also encouraged McKay to explore ways to scale the learning analytics fellows model. In partnership with U-M colleagues Jason Owen-Smith and Margaret Levenstein, McKay received a grant from the Sloan Foundation to extend across the Big Ten institutions the analysis his research group had completed as part of the LATF efforts (Koester, Grom, & McKay, 2016). Meeting in August 2014, the gathered attendees agreed on four research areas: (1) compare and contrast differences between students' incoming GPA and received grades in various course types, (2) explore course sequences and when students declare different majors, (3) investigate students' persistence within degree programs and differences across disciplines, and (4) examine how students engage in federally funded research projects and the courses students enroll in to participate in directed research. Participants reconvened in November 2014 to discuss preliminary results. As one example, five institutions reported similar results when investigating gendered performance differences in introductory STEM courses. Other projects being considered include how the Big Ten or other higher education consortia might collaboratively build a multi-institutional dataset providing a larger picture of the impact of research universities.

Another key project that took place during the LATF's charge was a $2 million grant from the National Science Foundation awarded to McKay and colleagues to support analytics-powered reform efforts in introductory physics, biology, chemistry, and mathematics courses. This project connected departmental teams and allowed them to reevaluate curricula, instructional modes, and other elements of the learning environments while carefully considering all the underlying data. As a result, using data to support pedagogical decisions in these departments has become the norm and is credited for making broad, and relatively fast, changes to foundational courses. The impact of these projects on the U-M community aligns closely with findings from similar projects undertaken at other Big Ten universities, as noted by colleagues at Purdue University: "the institutional application of analytics can result in a major shift for colleges and universities with regard to the culture fostered around undergraduate learning" (Pistilli, Willis, & Campbell, 2014, p. 88).

Finding New Homes for Continuing Learning Analytics Task Force Efforts

As the LATF's 3-year charge came to a close, the committee sought to institutionalize or find new homes for many of the efforts that successfully fostered the emergent learning analytics research community. In an effort to help scale the learning analytics fellows concept beyond U-M, McKay developed a massive open online course entitled Practical Learning Analytics, now available on the EdX platform. This course offers a flexible, collaborative introduction to learning analytics in higher education in which students learn by doing, using realistic data and code. Course materials are intended to support groups of faculty and staff who might create their own learning analytics fellows program.

Institutional support for new, innovating learning analytics projects has migrated to U-M's new Michigan Institute for Data Science (MIDAS). In June 2016, MIDAS announced that learning analytics was one of their four designated thrust areas and two new projects had been launched, one analyzing students' written work and behavioral data and the other investigating connections between students' values and beliefs and their success in higher education.

While MIDAS has been organized around research using data science techniques, the role for continuing a broad, faculty-led effort to investigate learning analytics issues and questions has been charged to the new U-M Institutional Learning Analytics (UMILA) group. Co-chaired by McKay and former U-M provost Paul Courant, UMILA consists of nine faculty members who work along with academic administrative leaders to identify the areas of learning analytics research that would most deeply influence decision making at administrative levels of the university.

Finally, the SLAM series, which had run for 4 years, has been reimagined as a working research group focused on methodological and technical issues in the Academic Innovation at Michigan Analytics series, supported by the new Office of Academic Innovation. This office also houses the new Digital Innovation Greenhouse, an incubator designed to broadly scale analytics-powered digital tools for teaching and learning. This new office, along with MIDAS and UMILA, has provided continuing institutional support for learning analytics and has begun to grow the community beyond the faculty, students, and staff who regularly attended the SLAM seminars.

Conclusion

The rise of scholarly research and institutionally actionable uses of learning analytics at the University of Michigan was built on a number of activities supported by key stakeholders. These include faculty leaders who engaged in related scholarly research, an IT infrastructure that provided access to necessary student-level data, an informed IRB and Office of General Council who helped guide the conditions for ethical use of the data under FERPA, and a central administration that provided financial support that allowed community building through public talks, a fellows program, and seed money for emerging projects. While an institution need not employ all of the various components and initiatives that U-M has supported thus far, these activities have been instrumental in building a broad and visible interdisciplinary community across a large research university.

The impact of this effort has been recognized beyond campus. In 2016, the Society for Learning Analytics Research (SoLAR) invited U-M to host their summer institute annually, and Teasley was elected to be the next president of the society. Regardless of the specific initiatives taken, academic institutions are well served by promoting the growth of a community of scholars and practitioners interested in leveraging institutional data to improve student learning. Engaging faculty and students to explore and uncover new insights in student learning can fundamentally transform the culture of a postsecondary institution toward continuous, evidence-informed improvement of teaching and learning processes.

References

Arnold, K. E., Lonn, S., & Pistilli, M. D. (2014). An exercise in institutional reflection: The Learning Analytics Readiness Instrument (LARI). In A. Pardo & S. Teasley (Eds.), *Proceedings from the Fourth International Conference on Learning Analytics and Knowledge* (pp. 163–167). New York, NY: ACM. https://doi.org/10.1145/2567574.2567621

Baepler, P., & Murdoch, C. J. (2010). Academic analytics and data mining in higher education. *International Journal for the Scholarship of Teaching and Learning, 4*(2), 1–9. doi: 10.20429/ijsotl.2010.040217

Brooks, C., Chavez, O., Tritz, J., & Teasley, S. D. (2015). Reducing selection bias in quasi-experimental educational studies. *Proceedings of the Fifth International Conference on Learning Analytics & Knowledge* (pp. 295–299). New York, NY: ACM. https://doi.org/10.1145/2723576.2723614

Cameron, K. S. (1984). Organizational adaptation and higher education. *Journal of Higher Education, 55*(2), 122–144. Retrieved from http://www.tandfonline.com/doi/abs/10.1080/00221546.1984.11778679

Center for Research on Learning and Teaching. (2017). Student Learning and Analytics at Michigan (SLAM). Retrieved from http://crlt.umich.edu/slam?tid%5B%5D=420

Freeman, S., O'Connor, E., Parks, J. W., Cunningham, M., Hurley, D. H., Haak, D., ... Wenderoth, M. P. (2007). Prescribed active learning increases performance in introductory biology. *CBE–Life Sciences Education, 6*(2), 132–139. https://doi.org/10.1187/cbe.06-09-0194

Koester, B. P., Grom, G., & McKay, T. A. (2016). Patterns of gendered performance difference in introductory STEM courses. Retrieved from https://arxiv.org/abs/1608.07565

Lonn, S., & Teasley, S. D. (2009). Saving time or innovating practice: Investigating perceptions and uses of learning management systems. *Computers & Education, 53*(3), 686–694. https://doi.org/10.1016/j.compedu.2009.04.008

McKay, T. A. (2012). The University of Michigan Learning Analytics Task Force: 2012–2015. Retrieved from https://sites.google.com/a/umich.edu/um-latf/

McKay, T. A., & Teasley, S. D. (2011). Rackham interdisciplinary seminar proposal: Academic analytics: Interdisciplinary data mining to improve student learning. Retrieved from http://hdl.handle.net/2027.42/134731

Miller, K. (2011). Gender matters: Assessing and addressing the persistent gender gap in physics education. University of Michigan Honors Senior Thesis. Retrieved from http://hdl.handle.net/2027.42/85304

Nam, S., Lonn, S., Brown, T., Davis, C. S., & Koch, D. (2014). Customized course advising: Investigating engineering student success with incoming profiles and patterns of concurrent course enrollment. *Proceedings of the Fourth International Conference on Learning Analytics and Knowledge* (pp. 16–25). New York, NY: ACM. https://doi.org/10.1145/2567574.2567589

Norris, D., Baer, L., & Offerman, M. (2009). A national agenda for action analytics. Paper presented at the National Symposium on Action Analytics, Minneapolis, MN, September. Retrieved from http://lindabaer.efoliomn.com/uploads/settinganationalagendaforactionanalytics101509.pdf

Pistilli, M. D., Willis, III, J. E., & Campbell, J. P. (2014). Analytics through an institutional lens: Definition, theory, design, and impact. In J. A. Larusson & B. White (Eds.),

Learning analytics: From research to practice (pp. 79–101). New York, NY: Springer. https://doi.org/10.1007/978-1-4614-3305-7_5

Shultz, G. V., Winschel, G. A., & Gottfried, A. (2015). The impact of general chemistry prerequisite on student achievement and progression to subsequent chemistry courses: A regression discontinuity analysis. *Journal of Chemical Education, 92*(9), 1449–1455. https://doi.org/10.1021/acs.jchemed.5b00209

Wright, M. C., McKay, T., Hershock, C., Miller, K., & Tritz, J. (2014). Better than expected: Using learning analytics to promote student success in gateway science. *Change: The Magazine of Higher Learning, 46*(1), 28–34. https://doi.org/10.1080/00091383.2014.867209

STEVEN LONN *is the Director of Enrollment Research and Data Management in the Office of Enrollment Management at the University of Michigan.*

TIMOTHY A. MCKAY *is an Arthur F. Thurnau Professor of Physics, Astronomy, and Education and the Faculty Director of the Digital Innovation Greenhouse at the University of Michigan.*

STEPHANIE D. TEASLEY *is a Research Professor in the School of Information and the Director of the Learning, Education, and Design Lab at the University of Michigan.*

6

To scale student success, institutions may want to consider treating students more as partners, not just as customers or intervention recipients. One way to do so is sharing behavioral and academic feedback data that helps nudge students into taking responsibility for learning. The following chapter is drawn from the author's dissertation work (Fritz, 2016).

Using Analytics to Nudge Student Responsibility for Learning

John Fritz

In Thaler and Sunstein's *Nudge* (2008), we learn how organizations can help people make better decisions "if they had paid full attention and possessed complete information, unlimited cognitive abilities, and complete self control" (p. 5). To achieve such an ambitious goal, the authors describe "choice architecture" as a way to design the environment or context to influence people's choices. For example, school children choose healthier foods if the cafeteria displays fruits before desserts, consumers better judge credit card offers if they can project their actual spending against proposed interest rates, and more drivers become organ donors if license renewal requires making a specific "yes" or "no" choice.

Thaler and Sunstein (2008) base choice architecture on a concept they define as "Libertarian Paternalism," two terms they admit work better together than they do alone. Basically, they believe people should be free to choose, but that

> It is legitimate for choice architects to try to influence people's behavior in order to make their lives longer, healthier and better ... In our understanding, a policy is "paternalistic" if it tries to influence choices in a way that will make chooser better off, *as judged by themselves*. (p. 5)

How might institutions use choice architecture to nudge students with the insights of learning analytics? Given concerns about potential false positives and varying levels of digital literacy, some may understandably question if students should directly receive predictions about their performance, or if intermediaries (e.g., academic advisors) should interpret their data.

NEW DIRECTIONS FOR HIGHER EDUCATION, no. 179, Fall 2017 © 2017 Wiley Periodicals, Inc.
Published online in Wiley Online Library (wileyonlinelibrary.com) • DOI: 10.1002/he.20244

However, since the still-maturing field of learning analytics is more often focused on prediction than intervention, how can it ever hope to scale unless we consider the possibility of including students as partners, to interpret and act on their own data? Instead of treating students as passive recipients of institutional interventions, can institutions consider students as enabled partners, by sharing data that might help them help themselves? This chapter explores examples, principles, and implications of student-focused choice architecture as a viable analytics intervention strategy and a fascinating form of human computer interaction.

Assumptions

Before exploring how some institutions are already employing choice architecture to nudge students, we should review some key assumptions. First, if we try to scale student success by treating students as partners, then we must assume they are capable of that responsibility. As Tinto (1993) reminds us, institutions cannot "absolve" students from "at least partial responsibility for their own education."

> To do so denies both the right of the individual to refuse education and the right of the institution to be selective in its judgments as to who should be further educated. More importantly, it runs counter to the essential notion that effective education requires that individuals take responsibility for their own learning. (p. 144)

While others have affirmed student responsibility for learning (Astin, 1993; Davis & Murrell, 1994; Fink, 2003; Pascarella & Terenzini, 2005; Weimer, 2002), this concept is often minimized or even overlooked when focusing on what higher education institutions can and should do to promote student success. On a basic level, focusing institutional strategy and resources on facilitating student responsibility for learning resonates for the simple reason of scalability. Even if institutions are blessed with the most conscientious and proactive of instructors and advisors, how can this approach ever hope to scale? At many institutions, there are simply more struggling students than faculty and staff who can monitor their progress, let alone intervene. Tinto and others cited above remind us there are two sides of the student success equation that must be worked simultaneously: what the institution and the student can and should do.

Second, while U.S. institutions have an ethical and legal obligation to protect student privacy, as called for in the Family Educational Rights and Privacy Act (FERPA), it is nonsensical to think that student identity should be hidden from the very faculty, staff, or administrators responsible for student success at the institutions where they are enrolled. Indeed, FERPA not only allows those with an "educational interest" to study the behavior of past students to improve the experience of current and future students, it

NEW DIRECTIONS FOR HIGHER EDUCATION • DOI: 10.1002/he

also empowers them to do so. Indeed, Campbell (2007; Campbell, Deblois, & Oblinger, 2007; Willis, Campbell, & Pistilli, 2013) has rightly and frequently raised a concern about an institution's ethical obligation of knowing something about its students, and acting on this knowledge. FERPA provides the mandate for answering this question—by allowing institutions to study their own student performance data—while also protecting student privacy from anyone who is not employed by the institution.

Finally, predicting who we think may fail is not the same as intervening with them in a way they can understand or do anything about. In 2016, Simon P. Newman was forced to resign as president of Mount St. Mary's University after he said faculty should "drown the bunnies" [at-risk students] who he thought were unlikely to succeed (Mangan & Desantis, 2016). While his instinct to save unprepared students the time and expense of gradually failing out of the institution may have initially appeared to be empathetic or prudent, it begged the question of why *his* students were admitted in the first place, and drew criticism regarding the methods he subsequently recommended—to expel them on the basis of a single point-in-time survey administered in the first three weeks of the their first semester.

A Case Study for Nudging Students at University of Maryland, Baltimore County

With choice architecture and these assumptions in mind, let us consider a case for why and how institutions might nudge student awareness and success, by studying the experience at the University of Maryland, Baltimore County (UMBC). Between 2007 and 2010, we observed that students earning a D or F tended to use our Blackboard (Bb) learning management system (LMS) about 40% less than students earning a C or higher (Fritz, 2011). Initially, this was based on a convenience sample of 131 courses, but given the consistency of this pattern, we wondered what might happen if we shared this information with students during the semester. To do so, in 2008, we used our campus portal, myUMBC, to develop and present a simple student feedback tool we called Check My Activity (CMA). In addition to displaying a list of each student's own courses, the CMA allowed students to compare their own LMS activity—including any clicks or hits—to an anonymous summary of course peers. Also, if instructors used the online grade book, students could compare their own activity with course peers earning the same, lower, or higher grade for any assignment (Fritz, 2010). Two years later, we reported that students using the CMA feedback tool in spring 2012 were nearly twice as likely to earn a C or higher than students who did not (Fritz, 2013). Perhaps feedback to students about their LMS use could redefine the LMS itself into a real-time indicator of student engagement, not just a static document repository for the syllabus, presentations, and readings that it has largely become in higher education.

After further analysis of the CMA in academic year 2013–2014, we learned more about how students were using it—or not. Specifically, after using logistic regression to control for other factors such as gender, race, high school GPA, SAT score, and Pell eligibility, the CMA's strength of relationship to GPA was decidedly mixed. First, the CMA was only used by about 54% of the students in the study sample consisting of 2,696 UMBC full-time freshmen and transfer students. Second, while CMA usage was statistically significant ($p < 0.001$), the strength of relationship between use of the tool and GPA dissipated after accounting for other variables. Specifically, students using the CMA were only about 1.5 times more likely to earn a C or better class grade, or 2.0 or better term GPA, compared to peers who did not use the CMA. Finally, there was no significant difference in the likelihood of earning a C or better class grade or 2.0 term GPA based on the amount of CMA usage (Fritz, 2016). This finding seemed especially counterintuitive since the amount of overall LMS usage was associated with students earning higher grades and term GPA.

While we have tweaked the CMA over the years, and likely will continue to do so, we've also heard several anecdotal reports that students value the CMA, including receiving numerous complaints when it is down for maintenance. Going forward, we plan to conduct a qualitative analysis to complement our quantitative approach, based on an opt-in feedback survey that has been in place since 2008 (see https://umbc.box.com/cmasurveydata). Among other things, when asked what the CMA showed them about their LMS activity, more than 40% of the nearly 200 student respondents to date have said they were "surprised how my activity compared with peers," 25% said "it confirmed what I already know about my own activity," and 17% said "I would need to use it more to determine its usefulness." In addition, more than 60% of respondents said they would be "more inclined" to use the CMA before future assignments are due, which we interpret as an indicator of students' willingness to take more responsibility for their own learning. Also, it is interesting to note that women are more than twice as likely to report using the CMA than are men.

Most recently, in summer of 2015, when our myUMBC campus portal developed a "profile sharing" function, and the ability to login with Facebook or Google, we included the CMA so that students could share their CMA profile with parents or anyone with a valid portal login. To be clear, the student always controls if and how much of their profile they want others to see, including the CMA, but reviews from parent orientation meetings have been overwhelmingly positive. It has not hurt that UMBC's vice provost for enrollment management—and mother of a UMBC student—runs these parent orientations and has shared her experiences: "Accessing my son's CMA is better than grades, which are final and can't change," says Yvette Mozie-Ross. "But with the CMA, it allows us to have an informed discussion of how engaged he is in his classes, and discuss changes he might need to make or how and where to get help. As a parent, I appreciate the insight the CMA affords as he takes these initial steps on his own" (Fritz, 2016, p. 169).

While some may understandably question if the CMA should be expanded to others when its effectiveness for students is still to be determined, this is a luxury we have as practitioners to follow our instincts for developing or improving a digital environment that gives students better insight into and support of their own efforts. We realize many researchers and practitioners may not have such an intervention laboratory with which to experiment, but our hope is that by risking and sharing lessons learned, others may be inspired to initiate their own interventions or constructively critique ours, so that collectively we can evolve our own practice of what constitutes good information technology (IT) in support of teaching and learning.

Finally, one lesson learned relates to the inevitable "build or buy" decision that any technology strategy must resolve, especially in an emerging field like learning analytics. UMBC considered investing further in our homegrown approach to learning analytics before adopting Blackboard's Analytics for Learn, the tool the company built to assess its own LMS. After *The Chronicle of Higher Education* featured our work (Young, 2009), we even released our code at the 2009 Bb World users conference, which a handful of other schools have downloaded and implemented (see http://www.umbc.edu/oit/newmedia/blackboard/stats/getthecode.php). It made more sense, however, to help influence Bb's approach—which more schools might use—than try to fund more resources to continue developing our own. Bb was amenable and the partnership helped us scale the exploration of LMS activity and grades that informed our "feedback as intervention" nudge that the CMA provides to students.

Other Notable Student-Facing Analytics Interventions

Since its inception in 2011, a recurring theme of the annual Learning Analytics and Knowledge conference is that the field needs to live up to its own definitions of analytics as "actionable intelligence," and move beyond prediction to implement and evaluate interventions (Fiaidhi, 2014). Toward this end, the following is a brief review of three other notable interventions that focus on student attention to—if not responsibility for—their own learning.

Course Signals (Purdue University). A year after John Campbell completed his dissertation (2007) and published findings in *Educause Review* (Campbell, Deblois, & Oblinger, 2007), *The Chronicle of Higher Education* rightly focused on Purdue's pioneering and innovative Course Signals intervention that could alert faculty of at-risk students (Rampell, 2008). Faculty could then alert their students by issuing a green (stay the course), yellow (caution), or red (jeopardy) traffic light signal when they logged into their Blackboard LMS course site. This same *Chronicle* article also reported on a 2005 study by the University of Georgia that showed student use of

NEW DIRECTIONS FOR HIGHER EDUCATION • DOI: 10.1002/he

the LMS alone was statistically significant in predicting student success in three online English, geography, and history courses (Morris, Finnegan, & Wu, 2005). Together, the Purdue and Georgia research established the LMS as a viable platform worthy of study for predictive analytics, but because researchers found that online LMS activity alone was highly predictive, the Georgia study was particularly promising for schools that might not have been able—like Purdue—to integrate LMS and student information system data for predictive analysis.

A few years later, Arnold (2010), published further evidence that Purdue's Course Signals was effective at not only predicting students in need of help, but also intervening to improve student success and institutional retention. Purdue eventually drew criticism about the validity of its year-to-year retention claims, though student performance improvements in Signals vs. non-Signals courses *during* a semester were never contested (Feldstein, 2014).

Arnold did acknowledge one concern: a lack of consistent, effective practice among faculty about if, when, and how to flip the signal alerting students they are in jeopardy. This is a key point: Signals does not alert students—it alerts the faculty member who then decides whether to display a red, yellow, or green alert. Despite Purdue's sophisticated predictive risk algorithm, how and when faculty flip the Signals intervention switch has varied, as it most likely would at any other institution that has such systems.

Key Signals developers Kim Arnold, John Campbell, and Matt Pistilli have since moved on to other institutions, but Purdue's Course Signals helped define and raise the bar of learning analytics practice by implementing a plausible, systemic intervention.

ECoach (University of Michigan). Developed at the University of Michigan, Electronic Expert Coach (originally E2Coach, now simply ECoach) is a recommendation engine designed to help current students pass difficult courses by providing feedback and advice from peers who performed "better than expected" in a prior version of the same course (McKay, Miller, & Tritz, 2012). Specifically, ECoach is based on a proven tailoring and targeted communication model developed by the Centers for Disease Control and used by public health professionals to match people who need to change their behavior by sharing messages from peers who did. Advice is collected through interviews with students who have done well in a course, particularly if they did "better than expected" (based on analysis of precollege demographics, GPA, SAT, etc.). Faculty members are interviewed as well, but the focus is based more on the value of authentic peer-to-peer feedback. Once gathered, ECoach presents prior successful students' habits and strategies in the form of opt-in, on-demand, and tailored advice to currently struggling students in the same course. By matching student demographics and key course milestones (for example assignments, quizzes, exams), the currently enrolled struggling students can opt in to get advice and tips from successful peers who share similar demographics, and at key times in the semester when they may be facing challenges understanding or applying course concepts.

As is often found with these types of support initiatives, many of the "better than expected" students ended up using the support resources the university was all too ready and willing to provide. By contrast, weaker or "worse than expected" students don't always avail themselves of needed supports, and getting authentic advice from peers to do so is more likely to be effective. ECoach was initially developed to help students pass introductory physics, but has since been expanded to many STEM courses.

Degree Compass (Austin Peay State University). Degree Compass has been shown to be an effective intervention for the problem of inefficient student course registration and "time-to-degree" completion (Denley, 2012, 2013). Specifically, by studying the demographics, academic preparation, final grades, and course registration choices of past students, Degree Compass helps current students by recommending courses in which they are more likely to succeed. A customized "Reverse Degree Audit" algorithm generates a five-star recommendation based on general education requirements, major requirements, and a student's predicted grade, which has been shown to be 92% accurate in terms of predicting actual passing grades of C or better. Degree Compass does not take into account the faculty course design or student effort in the LMS course per se, but given the accuracy of grade prediction, and a recent push to redesign key gateway courses, Austin Peay is in a better position to identify and support students who are likely to struggle from the start.

Discussion: Leveraging Information Technology–Facilitated Peer Pressure

In a way, each of the examples above illustrates how the principles of choice architecture could be used to leverage student responsibility for learning. In particular, they all share the user's behavioral or academic data with the student, to raise awareness about where he or she currently stands, and directly or indirectly present optimal choices to consider, especially in the ECoach context of what peers might have done already or are likely to do.

Why might comparison with successful peers be effective? Basically, a self-regulated and self-directed learner is one who can self-judge and take responsibility for doing all he or she can to close a perceived gap in performance compared to a peer or exemplar, but successful peers can help raise awareness that a gap exists. Indeed, from a cognitive psychology perspective, research on self-regulated learning shows how the discrepancy between successful and struggling peers might inspire and model necessary and very specific changes in behavior (Zimmerman, Bandura, & Martinez-Pons, 1992; Zimmerman & Schunk, 2001). Similarly, the work on self-efficacy (Bandura, 1986, 1997) shows how belief in one's ability and actions to affect change can inspire or sustain such effort exhibited by others, while the research on the implications of a growth versus fixed mindset suggests that intelligence is not fixed at birth, but can be developed through hard work and effort (Dweck, 2007). As the old adage goes, nobody learns from a position of comfort. It is not until we find our current knowledge, skills, and abilities to be wanting—perhaps especially if compared to peers, role models, or exemplars we wish to emulate—that we can begin the necessary first step of wanting to change our status quo. By extension, institutional technology systems that support teaching and learning can be designed to accentuate this process of self-awareness through peer and exemplar comparison.

This social comparison is not unlike the "crowdsourcing" and "quantified self" dynamics that our students experience in a myriad of consumer sites using some form of "big data" dashboard or feedback to help make people more aware of their own behavior or choices in relation to others. For example, monthly bills from utility companies now display each customer's energy consumption compared to the average of one's neighbors. Similarly, the online finance site Mint.com lets you compare your spending on items like gas and groceries with other, anonymous Mint.com users in your city, state, or even across the country. Several fitness sites like Run Keeper, Map My Run, or My Fitness Pal let you do the same.

It's not enough anymore for a vendor to simply advertise their service through old-fashioned, one-way mass marketing. Increasingly, consumers are expecting to be able to interact with data, either through an overlay of their own data with that of others, or by connecting with trusted sources to help benchmark behaviors or proposed goods and services. People want a way to see themselves in the context of a larger whole. This is the essence of crowd sourcing. Why should it be any different in higher education?

Conclusion

To date, the learning analytics field has been characterized more by a focus on prediction than intervention. There are several reasons why this is the case, including the considerable effort to build a big data infrastructure, an understandable desire to perfect predictions before acting on them, and a preoccupation with scaling potential interventions, so we can be as efficient and effective in our efforts to improve student success.

However, there are three compelling reasons to treat students as agents of change in their own academic welfare: (1) responsibility for learning is what makes someone a student and not a customer; (2) paternalism does not scale: there are simply more students than there are institutional caretakers such as teachers, advisors, and educational administrators; and (3) institutions have an ethical obligation to share what they think they know about current students based on the experiences of prior students.

The examples provided in this chapter illustrate how we might go about nudging students, not only to raise awareness about and leverage their responsibility for learning, but also to pursue a more scalable approach to student success. While many affirm that students should be responsible for their learning, the implications for pedagogical practice of course hinge on whether we believe students are capable and motivated to do so.

Weimer (2002) is unequivocal that student responsibility is "theirs alone" and even devotes an entire chapter to the subject. Recalling a colleague's twist on the old "can't lead a horse to water" adage—saying "it was the teacher's job to put salt in the oats"—Weimer says "it is clear our responsibility is to take explicit actions that will motivate student learning. The horse who has had salt put in his oats does not have to be forced to drink. He is thirsty, knows he is thirsty, and is looking for water" (p. 103).

Nudging students with and about their own learning data, especially in the context of higher performing peers they wish to emulate, may be one of the most scalable ways we can salt the horse's oats.

References

Arnold, K. (2010). Signals: Applying academic analytics. *EDUCAUSE Quarterly, 33*(1). Retrieved from http://www.educause.edu/library/EQM10110

Astin, A. W. (1993). *What matters in college? Four critical years revisited. Jossey-Bass Higher and Adult Education Series.* San Francisco, CA: Jossey-Bass. Retrieved from http://www.eric.ed.gov/ERICWebPortal/detail?accno=ED351927

Bandura, A. (1986). *Social foundations of thought at action: A social cognitive theory.* Englewood Cliffs, NJ: Prentice-Hall.

Bandura, A. (1997). *Self-efficacy: The exercise of control.* New York, NY: W. H. Freeman.

Campbell, J. (2007). *Utilizing student data within the course management system to determine undergraduate student academic success: An exploratory study* (Doctoral dissertation). Retrieved from http://proquest.umi.com/pqdweb?did=1417816411&Fmt=7& clientId=11430&RQT=309&VName=PQD

Campbell, J., Deblois, P., & Oblinger, D. (2007, August). Academic analytics: A new tool for a new era. *EDUCAUSE Review, 42*(4), 40–57. Retrieved from http://www. educause.edu/EDUCAUSE±Review/EDUCAUSEReviewMagazineVolume42/Academ icAnalyticsANewToolforaN/161749

Davis, T. M., & Murrell, P. H. (1994). Turning teaching into learning. The role of student responsibility in the collegiate experience. *ERIC Digest.* Retrieved from http://eric .ed.gov/?q=Turning±Teaching±into±Learning%3a±+The±Role±of±Student±Res ponsibility±in±the±Collegiate±Experience±&id=ED372702

Denley, T. (2012, September 5). Austin Peay State University: Degree Compass. *EDUCAUSE Review.* Retrieved from http://www.educause.edu/ero/article/austin-peay-state-university-degree-compass

Denley, T. (2013). *Degree Compass course recommendation system* (Case Study) (p. 5). Educause Learning Initiative. Retrieved from http://net.educause.edu/ir/library/ eli_so/SEI1303.pdf

Dweck, C. (2007). *Mindset: The new psychology of success.* New York, NY: Random House Digital.

Feldstein, M. (2014, July 14). *NPR and missed (Course) Signals.* Retrieved from http://mfeldstein.com/npr-missed-course-signals/

Fiaidhi, J. (2014). The next step for learning analytics. *IT Professional, 16*(5), 4–8. https://doi.org/10.1109/MITP.2014.78

Fink, L. D. (2003). *Creating significant learning experiences: An integrated approach to designing college courses.* San Francisco, CA: Jossey-Bass.

Fritz, J. (2010). Video demo of UMBC's "Check My Activity" tool for students. *EDUCAUSE Quarterly, 33*(4). Retrieved from http://www.educause.edu/library/EQM1049

Fritz, J. (2011). Classroom walls that talk: Using online course activity data of successful students to raise self-awareness of underperforming peers. *The Internet and Higher Education, 14*(2), 89–97. https://doi.org/10.1016/j.iheduc.2010.07.007

Fritz, J. (2013). *Using analytics at UMBC: Encouraging student responsibility and identifying effective course designs* (Research Bulletin) (p. 11). Louisville, CO: Educause Center for Applied Research. Retrieved from http://www.educause.edu/library/ resources/using-analytics-umbc-encouraging-student-responsibility-and-identifying -effective-course-designs

Fritz, J. (2016). *Using analytics to encourage student responsibility for learning and identify course designs that help* (Doctoral dissertation). University of Maryland, Baltimore County. Retrieved from http://search.proquest.com.proxy-bc.researchport.umd. edu/pqdtlocal1005865/docview/1795528531/abstract/8BFCC74B55A94651PQ/1

Mangan, K., & Desantis, N. (2016, March 1). Simon Newman resigns as president of Mount St. Mary's. *The Chronicle of Higher Education.* Retrieved from http://www. chronicle.com/article/Simon-Newman-Resigns-as/235541/

McKay, T., Miller, K., & Tritz, J. (2012). What to do with actionable intelligence: E²Coach as an intervention engine. In *Proceedings of the 2nd International Conference on Learning Analytics and Knowledge* (pp. 88–91). New York, NY: ACM. https://doi. org/10.1145/2330601.2330627

Morris, L. V., Finnegan, C., & Wu, S.-S. (2005). Tracking student behavior, persistence, and achievement in online courses. *The Internet and Higher Education, 8*(3), 221–231. https://doi.org/10.1016/j.iheduc.2005.06.009

Pascarella, E. T., & Terenzini, P. T. (2005). *How college affects students: A third decade of research.* San Francisco, CA: Jossey-Bass.

Rampell, C. (2008, May 30). Colleges mine data to predict dropouts. *The Chronicle of Higher Education.* Retrieved from http://chronicle.com/article/Colleges-Mine-Data -to-Predict/22141/

Thaler, R. H., & Sunstein, C. R. (2008). *Nudge: Improving decisions about health, wealth, and happiness.* New Haven, CT: Yale University Press.

Tinto, V. (1993). *Leaving college: Rethinking the causes and cures of student attrition* (2nd ed.). Chicago, IL: University of Chicago Press.

Weimer, M. (2002). *Learner-centered teaching: Five key changes to practice.* San Francisco, CA: Jossey-Bass.

Willis, J., Campbell, J., & Pistilli, M. (2013, May 6). Ethics, big data, and analytics: A model for application. *EDUCAUSE Review.* Retrieved from http://er.educause.edu/articles/2013/5/ethics-big-data-and-analytics-a-model-for-app lication

Young, J. (2009, January 8). A wired way to rate professors—and connect teachers. *The Chronicle of Higher Education.* Retrieved from http://chronicle.com/article/ A-Wired-Way-to-Rate-Profess/1439/

Zimmerman, B. J., Bandura, A., & Martinez-Pons, M. (1992). Self-motivation for academic attainment: The role of self-efficacy beliefs and personal goal setting. *American Educational Research Journal, 29*(3), 663–676. https://doi.org/10.3102/ 00028312029003663

Zimmerman, B. J., & Schunk, D. H. (2001). *Self-regulated learning and academic achievement: Theoretical perspectives.* Mahwah, NJ: Erlbaum.

JOHN FRITZ is the Associate Vice President of Instructional Technology in the Division of Information Technology for University of Maryland, Baltimore County.

NEW DIRECTIONS FOR HIGHER EDUCATION • DOI: 10.1002/he

The many complex challenges posed by learning analytics can best be understood within a framework of structural justice, which focuses on the ways in which the informational, operational, and organizational structures of learning analytics influence students' capacities for self-development and self-determination. This places primary responsibility for ethical use of learning analytics on institutions rather than on users.

Ethics and Justice in Learning Analytics

Jeffrey Alan Johnson

The explosion of learning analytics raises deep questions about whether it can be done ethically. There are many complex challenges posed by learning analytics, ranging from widely acknowledged concerns about privacy to less well understood concerns with methodology. This chapter suggests that these concerns can best be understood within a framework of structural justice, which focuses on the ways in which the informational, operational, and organizational structures of learning analytics influence students' capacities for self-development and self-determination. This structural perspective can inform analytics practitioners and encourage a more sophisticated design that moderates these concerns, but largely shifts the focus of concern from individual users of learning analytics to the institutions that control the structural context within which they are implemented.

Ethical Questions in Learning Analytics

Learning analytics presents a complex array of ethical challenges. These challenges are easy to subsume under a simple notion of ethical action, but complexity emerges quickly. In part, it emerges simply because the challenges are often problems of unintended consequences, and from the fact that the challenges can weigh against each other. Complexity also emerges because these challenges are often driven not by the kinds of choices about action usually addressed by professional ethics codes, but by beliefs about data science itself that hide the ethical choices in learning analytics behind a belief in technological neutrality and information objectivity. One can point to at least four major ethical concerns in learning analytics: (1) privacy, (2) individuality, (3) autonomy, and (4) discrimination.

NEW DIRECTIONS FOR HIGHER EDUCATION, no. 179, Fall 2017 © 2017 Wiley Periodicals, Inc.
Published online in Wiley Online Library (wileyonlinelibrary.com) • DOI: 10.1002/he.20245

Privacy. The most visible challenge related to learning analytics is privacy. Most commonly, privacy is understood in terms of information flows (Nissenbaum, 2010): privacy rights are protected by preventing information from moving from those who hold it legitimately to those who have no right to such information. This, it would seem at first glance, is a minor consideration in learning analytics, as information either does not flow at all (the institution's information never leaves the institution) or flows from the institution to a vendor acting as an agent of the institution. The strongest concern has been the flow of information to vendors who combine institutions' data for analysis, such as the controversial InBloom project in secondary education (Singer, 2014). InBloom used data from primary and secondary schools to build general predictive models that schools could then use to better predict student outcomes. Parents objected to InBloom's access to sensitive student data such as attendance, discipline, and disability regardless of the use to which it was to be put: InBloom's mere acquisition of the data was seen as intrusive. But this is a quite narrow view of both information flows and privacy. In some cases, learning analytics are inferring information about students that the students themselves would be reluctant to divulge to either the institution or an individual faculty member, essentially creating an electronic reputation that a student may not want to precede them into the classroom. Arizona State University, for example, developed a system to predict students who intended to transfer (Parry, 2012). To the extent that consent is an essential feature of privacy, these would be privacy violations even though information flowed only from one campus data system to another.

Individuality. The recognition of student individuality is also problematic in learning analytics. Learning analytics does not act on human beings. Rather, it *creates* beings composed of distinct bundles of information meant to correspond with human beings, what Floridi (2010) calls "interconnected information organisms, or *inforgs*" (p. 9, emphasis in original). Here, in fact, is one of the great advantages of learning analytics: while traditional statistics reduces all students to the central tendency (whether of a set of variables individually as in descriptive statistics or of a relationship among variables as in inferential statistics), the big data techniques behind learning analytics can treat each case individually, recognizing its uniqueness and allowing analysis of the diversity of cases (Two Crows Corporation, 2005).

But learning analytics may present the opposite challenge, disaggregating students into unrelated characteristics. For example, a decision tree model used by one large state university to predict retention classified students first by grade point average and then by whether they had visited their advisor. The prediction was useful, but it is likely that these two characteristics are not distinct; a discursive or ethnographic lens might reveal them as part of an identity in which the students see themselves as students (rather than, for example, as workers who are taking classes to advance) and thus take continued enrollment for granted (rather than consciously deciding whether to enroll for each semester). This dehumanization is then imposed on the students as institutional decisions are made based not on humanistic complexes of individual and social meaning but on mechanical processes of measurement, classification, and response. The institution may require that all students must see their advisors before enrolling in order to move students to an apparently more successful classification. The analytics process that seems to point to concrete, actionable information that can help students succeed may have the opposite effect, reinforcing a nonstudent identity that is an obstacle to success for those who struggle to maintain a high GPA and see their advisors regularly.

Autonomy. In principle, students are understood to be adults, autonomous individuals who can critically think and act to further their own good. Learning analytics can be deeply challenging to this autonomy. Rarely are such systems outright coercive, but one could imagine developing such systems by, for instance, linking student activity data from a learning management system to financial aid awards. Rather than relying on end-of-semester grades, an institution might condition aid on keeping up on work performed over the course of the semester: reading materials accessed, assignments completed, and so forth. In conjunction with an "Aid Like a Paycheck" disbursement schedule (Ware, Weissman, & McDermott, 2013), this would essentially condition students' immediate ability to meet their financial needs on compliance with course requirements.

More common than fully coercive systems are those that operate more paternalistically. Austin Peay State University adopted a course recommendation system based on the belief that students made poor choices regarding which classes to take (Parry, 2012). The system considered student performance in previous courses, and recommended courses that would maximize students' GPA and thus their likelihood of maintaining scholarships and of graduating. This system was designed to counter perceived lack of information and laziness among students that led (in the view of the administration) to unwise choices. The solution is for the institution to make choices for the students, steering them to the wise decision at the expense of their autonomy. A more complex version of this uses the control of minutiae and the possibility of constant surveillance—core features of the typical marriage of LMS and analytics suite—to create a disciplinary environment (Foucault, 1995) in which the structure of the situation leads students to comply with the institution's preferences on their own. Systems that classify students on their course activity and communicate that classification to the student and the instructor (Parry, 2011) operate within a framework of disciplinary power rather than a classically coercive one, but nonetheless severely constrain student autonomy and agency.

Discrimination. One of the emerging issues in big data more broadly is its potential for "algorithmic discrimination." Biases in data and in the social practices underlying it are increasingly seen as incorporating bias into analytics processes. As Cegłowski (2016, para 14) puts it, "We have turned to machine learning, an ingenious way of disclaiming responsibility for anything. Machine learning is like money laundering for bias." A series of ProPublica investigations have found that the same algorithm, trained on data from a variety of different news sources, produced wildly different results. When the algorithm used by Google to identify synonyms for searches is trained on data from websites of the left-leaning *Huffington Post* and *The Nation*, the most common search synonym for "BlackLivesMatter" is "hashtag" (that is, one receives results for both "BlackLivesMatter" and "BlackLivesMatter hashtag"). But when trained on data from the right-leaning *Daily Caller* and *Breitbart* it is "AllLivesMatter," an antonym rather than a synonym for the original search.

Thus when a search is executed, the differently trained algorithms will generate different search results (Larson, Angwin, & Parris, 2016). Both algorithms will show results presenting claims of institutionalized racism in the criminal justice system made by the Black Lives Matter movement. But the conservatively trained algorithm automatically replies that "All Lives Matter," a reply originally crafted to discredit the arguments of the movement, while the liberally trained one will lead to social media that present a widespread, grassroots social movement that may or may not be representative of activism offline. In either case, the training data has given the algorithm a form of political agency. This can be deliberate, but it need not be.

The ProPublica investigations also found that Asians were twice as likely to be offered a higher than average price for Princeton Review SAT prep courses, which the company argues is an incidental effect of its geographic pricing algorithm (Angwin, Mattu, & Larson, 2015). In this case, geography became an effective proxy for race, producing a disparate effect presumably without intentional discrimination. These effects, Scholes (2016) argues, are readily seen in learning analytics as well, especially where group membership is used to predict risk scores. She contends that effective instructional design can mitigate these risks by designing analytics around effort measurements and dynamic factors. While this is laudable as an effort to overcome demographic discrimination, the recent debate over the nature of "grit" as a character trait promoting success suggests effort measures are no better. As reviewed recently by Ris (2015), grit is alternately seen as precisely the kind of dynamic, effort-based measure that Scholes advocates or as a product of a safe, White, privileged upbringing (for example, Calarco, 2014) in which opportunities to recover from failure abound, making it a proxy for traditional race and class in victim-blaming explanations for failure. To the extent that the latter is true, using an instrument that measures grit in an algorithm (for instance, that used by Mount St. Mary's College in its now-infamous "drown the bunnies" fiasco) writes racial discrimination into educational practices by laundering it through "a clean, mathematical apparatus that gives the status quo the aura of logical inevitability" (Cegłowski, 2016, para. 14).

None of this is to say that learning analytics are inherently unethical. Rather, it suggests two key points about ethics in learning analytics: (1) that learning analytics are not simply value-neutral math based on objective data, and thus (2) that ethical learning analytics is not just a matter of good faith. Each time an analytics system is implemented, implementers face unavoidable ethical questions. For example, autonomy is a paramount value in American society, but there are some circumstances in which it can be violated. One must therefore answer the question of whether a particular implementation of learning analytics violates autonomy and, if so, whether the particular violation is permissible. One must then ask whether the data chosen to underlie the algorithm on which the intervention is based are more than just the biases of the collectors and analysts. And one must question whether other values might take precedence over autonomy, as an absolute claim for the primacy of autonomy (or privacy, or efficiency, etc.) is by no means uncontroversial. To raise these questions is not to criticize learning analytics and argue for a blanket injunction against the field. Questions like these are inherent in every analytics process and must be answered uniquely in each case.

From Ethics to Justice

The second key point raised by the ethical nature of learning analytics is that the answers given to the questions raised in the previous section require justification, not just assurances of good faith. The best source for such justification is found not in the myriad ethical considerations one might examine, but rather in a coherent conception of justice, as justice is especially attuned to complex tradeoffs among multiple values. Philosophers have taken two approaches to justice. The most common, *distributive justice*, considers the institutions and practices of a community (which would include, for many philosophers, voluntary associational relationships like higher education institutions) to be just if they reflect a just distribution of material and moral goods (for example, rights, liberties, or authority). However, Young (1990) argues that distributive approaches are inadequate when the question is one of relationships among people or groups rather than material goods. Such approaches fail to understand how social institutions shape "action, decisions about action, and provision of the means to develop and exercise capacities" (p. 16); these are as much a consequence of structural factors as they are distributions of material and moral goods. Instead, Young presents a structural theory of justice: a community is just to the extent that social structures and relationships facilitate both the capacity to develop and exercise its members' human capacities and their participation in determining their actions (respectively, self-development and self-determination).

NEW DIRECTIONS FOR HIGHER EDUCATION • DOI: 10.1002/he

This standard is, of course, not easy to meet. There are always some constraints on self-development and self-determination; especially in education, structural justice is constrained by the sometimes inherent conflict between the two. Most pedagogical approaches assume that learning requires systematic guidance, and thus deny students self-determination in order to further their capacities for self-development. Moreover, the two considerations are mutually constructive. Perrotta and Williamson (2016) show that "methods used for the classification and measurement of online education are partially involved in the creation of the realities they claim to measure" (p. 2). Students exist as students in part because we choose to measure them as students. At many institutions, for instance, continuing education students are not included in reported enrollment data. All institutions exclude non-degree-seeking students when reporting graduation rates to the federal Integrated Postsecondary Education Data System (IPEDS), but they report such students separately for IPEDS enrollment data. These decisions shape who institutions think of—and plan for—when they refer to their students as well as which attendees at the institution think of themselves as students. The decision of whom to count as students plays a substantial role in creating the identity of "student." As such, learning analytics, like all educational practices, does not just constrain or facilitate self-development or self-determination; it in fact contributes to the creation of the selves that seek development and determination.

Structural justice is a far more complex form of justice than distributive justice, matching the complexity of the underlying relationships it seeks to evaluate. Most structural approaches to justice thus argue not for a particular distribution of self-development and self-determination but directly against social structures that limit these. Such approaches see justice as a political rather than analytical process, that is, as the outcome of a negotiation among conflicting groups, not a legalistic application of specific rules.

Justice in Analytics

Ethical learning analytics, then, can be achieved by giving attention to the attendant structural conditions that determine how analytics furthers the self-development and self-determination of those involved, considering especially that of the students to whom the institution has its chief responsibility. There are at least four major kinds of structures to be considered in learning analytics: (1) the problem-model-intervention nexus, (2) the data translation regime, (3) the scientism and hyperpositivism of the analytic methods, and (4) the organizations that implement learning analytics.

The Problem-Model-Intervention Nexus.   When discussing ethics in learning analytics, there is a tendency to focus immediately on the expected intervention: Is it just to use learning analytics to "drown the bunnies ... put a Glock to their heads" as Mount St. Mary's College President Simon Newman described it (Svrluga, 2016)? This obscures the deeper operational structures involved in learning analytics. An analytics process is part of a nexus in which problems, analytics data and models, and interventions mutually support and inform each other. A noncognitive assessment may well be an unjust means of determining which students should be dismissed even if the intervention itself is not, but this is superficial, failing to uncover the deeper drivers of the problem. The two together, combined with a problem of needing to dismiss students before federal reporting deadlines, reveal a structural relationship. If the problem is encouraging students who will fail to not waste their time and effort, the noncognitive assessment may be helpful. But dismissing students *after* their arrival on campus is counterproductive to this statement of the problem. Viewing the nexus of problem, model, and intervention reveals that the problem is primarily the institution's responsibility to resource efficiency rather than to students. Indeed, the problem and the anticipated intervention is necessary to give meaning to the analytics: A predictive score is a cause for action because it classifies students in a way that allows the intervention to solve the particular problem.

The Data Translation Regime.   Contrary to common views, data is not an objective representation of reality (Johnson, 2013, 2015). Data is created as data systems select one representation from among the many representations possible. The U.S. Office of Management and Budget race and ethnicity framework used in IPEDS and other federal data collection systems is one of many possible ways of coding race and ethnicity; IPEDS data thus represents not an objective representation of the racial and ethnic composition of an institution's students but rather a translation of that composition into an official data state that stands in contrast to other data states excluded by the official data standards. The technical structures of a data system constitute a translation regime that substantively determines the content of the data used in analytics processes. That regime is a structure laden with questions of justice, such as the recognition of particular racial or ethnic groups, which in turn allows such groups to be represented in—or excluded from—decision making by being included in or excluded from the data (Johnson, 2016).

Scientism and Hyperpositivism.   The broader structural context of analytics algorithms themselves is built on the assumption that predictive learning analytics is, in fact, predictive. This belief is upheld in many cases by *scientism*, the ideology that science is the only path to true knowledge and that scientific knowledge is inherently and unquestionably objective (Hyslop-Margison & Naseem, 2007; Peterson, 2003). In predictive analytics, scientism especially reflects an extreme version of traditional positivist science. Observation and law-like generalization are foundational to information science in spite of decades of challenges to this approach in the social sciences and education. It is, for example, common for analytics reports to quote naïve error rates rather than proportional reduction in error measures and to attribute causation even when using models that do not support causal interpretation (Baradwaj & Pal, 2011; Delavari, Phon-Amnuaisuk, & Beizadeh, 2008; Llorente & Morant, 2011; Parry, 2012; Thomas & Galambos, 2004; Vialardi, Bravo, Shafti, & Ortigosa, 2009) in order to demonstrate apparent scientific rigor. Model choice depends on assumptions about reality and intent, but these are rarely interrogated because of hyperpositivist beliefs about the efficacy of predictive analytics. These structures present questions of justice, for instance by conferring intellectual authority on developers while shutting down critical inquiry with flippant injunctions against arguing with facts and dismissive contrasts between sound data and unfounded instinct. We assume our methods tell us which bunnies to drown, and those who suggest otherwise are denied the legitimacy of their claims by structures of knowledge.

Implementing Organizations.   The decisions about how to implement learning analytics take place in organizational structures. Within institutions, these structures often leave students entirely uninvolved or only include often unrepresentative student organizations. Beyond the institutions themselves the political economy of learning analytics both situates systems within intellectual property law that makes them "black boxes" opaque to examination and, as development is often a commercialization of one institution's system, makes generalizability an assumption rather than demonstrating it. Political and economic power thus reinforce scientism. The failure to examine these structures makes an ethics-only approach likely to fail. For example, although Boon (2016) recommends sharing data with students to empower them in informed, data-driven decision making and involves students directly in decisions about learning analytics, much of the student involvement in her model takes place in an environment that has already been strongly constrained by institutional decisions and systems. Students have a modicum of autonomy within a much deeper system of constraint that makes "informed decision making" much more a matter of institutionally driven disciplinarity.

Conclusion

Ethical learning analytics remains a significant challenge. Careful attention to five factors can help institutions further students' self-determination and self-development rather than building pseudoscientific caste systems for higher education that solidify and legitimize social stratification:

1. Intent. Is the intent of the learning analytics system to further students' self-determination and self-development or promote the institution's educational mission, rather than to promote the narrower self-interest of the institution?
2. Process. Is the process of developing a learning analytics system a broad negotiation among those affected?

3. Transparency. Can the whole of the problem-model-intervention nexus be understood and its assumptions examined? Are some parts of the process privileged from question (e.g., is the analytic model black-boxed)?
4. Data. Is the data a valid representation of the conditions at issue rather than either a representation driven by needs unrelated to the problem-model-intervention or a proxy for conditions that should be excluded?
5. Model. Is the connection between problem and intervention one that is amenable to prediction on an individual level without oversimplifying assumptions, scientism, or high-stakes errors?

Unfortunately, the analysis above suggests that the scope for individual practitioners to influence analytics toward more ethical approaches is limited. The well-noted ethical concerns are most often a consequence of the operational, informational, intellectual, and organizational structures of learning analytics. Ethical learning analytics must be an institutional concern.

References

Angwin, J., Mattu, S., & Larson, J. (2015, September 1). The tiger mom tax: Asians are nearly twice as likely to get a higher price from Princeton Review. *ProPublica*. Retrieved from https://www.propublica.org/article/asians-nearly-twice-as-likely-to-get-higher-price-from-princeton-review

Baradwaj, B. K., & Pal, S. (2011). Mining educational data to analyze students' performance. *International Journal of Advanced Computer Science and Applications*, 2(6), 63–69.

Boon, R. (2016, November). *Sharing data with students to inform decision making*. Association for Institutional Research. Retrieved from https://www.airweb.org/eAIR/askeair/Pages/Rachel-Boon.aspx

Calarco, J. M. (2014). Coached for the classroom: Parents' cultural transmission and children's reproduction of educational inequalities. *American Sociological Review*, 79(5), 1015–1037.

Cegłowski, M. (2016). *The moral economy of tech*. Text remarks from panel presented at the 28th SASE Annual Meeting, Berkeley, CA. Retrieved from http://idlewords.com/talks/sase_panel.htm

Delavari, N., Phon-Amnuaisuk, S., & Beizadeh, M. R. (2008). Data mining application in higher learning institutions. *Informatics in Education*, 7(1), 31–54.

Floridi, L. (2010). *Information: A very short introduction*. New York, NY: Oxford University Press.

Foucault, M. (1995). *Discipline and punish: The birth of the prison* (2nd ed.). New York, NY: Vintage Books.

Hyslop-Margison, E. J., & Naseem, M. A. (2007). *Scientism and education empirical research as neo-liberal ideology*. Dordrecht, Netherlands: Springer. Retrieved from http://public.eblib.com/EBLPublic/PublicView.do?ptiID=337528

Johnson, J. A. (2013). *Rendering students legible: Translation regimes and student identity in higher educational data systems*. Paper presented at the Annual Meeting of the Western Political Science Association, Seattle, WA.

Johnson, J. A. (2015). Information systems and the translation of transgender. *TSQ: Transgender Studies Quarterly*, 2(1), 160–165.

Johnson, J. A. (2016). Representing "Inforgs" in data-driven decisions. In J. Daniels, K. Gregory, & T. McMillan-Cottom (Eds.), *Digital sociologies*. Bristol, UK: Policy Press.

Larson, J., Angwin, J., & Parris, T. Jr. (2016, October 19). Breaking the black box: How machines learn to be racist. *ProPublica*. Retrieved from https://www.propublica. org/article/breaking-the-black-box-how-machines-learn-to-be-racist?word=blackliv esmatter

Llorente, R., & Morant, M. (2011). Data mining in higher education. In K. Funatsu (Ed.), *New fundamental technologies in data mining* (pp. 201–220). New York, NY: InTech.

Nissenbaum, H. (2010). *Privacy in context: Technology, policy, and the integrity of social life.* Stanford, CA: Stanford Law Books.

Parry, M. (2011, December 11). Colleges mine data to tailor students' experience. *The Chronicle of Higher Education*. Retrieved from https://chronicle.com/article/ A-Moneyball-Approach-to/130062/

Parry, M. (2012, July 18). College degrees, designed by the numbers. *The Chronicle of Higher Education*. Retrieved from https://chronicle.com/article/College-Degrees-Designed-by/132945/

Perrotta, C., & Williamson, B. (2016). The social life of learning analytics: Cluster analysis and the "performance" of algorithmic education. *Learning, Media and Technology*, 1–14. https://doi.org/10.1080/17439884.2016.1182927

Peterson, G. R. (2003). Demarcation and the scientistic fallacy. *Zygon*, 38(4), 751–761.

Ris, E. W. (2015). Grit: A short history of a useful concept. *Journal of Educational Controversy*, 10(1), Article 3.

Scholes, V. (2016). The ethics of using learning analytics to categorize students on risk. *Educational Technology Research and Development*, 64(5), 939–955.

Singer, N. (2014, April 22). InBloom student data repository to close. *New York Times*, p. B2.

Svrluga, S. (2016, January 19). University president allegedly says struggling freshmen are bunnies that should be drowned. *Washington Post*. Retrieved from https://www.washingtonpost.com/news/grade-point/wp/2016/01/19/university-presi dent-allegedly-says-struggling-freshmen-are-bunnies-that-should-be-drowned-that-a -glock-should-be-put-to-their-heads/

Thomas, E., & Galambos, N. (2004). What satisfies students? Mining student-opinion data with regression and decision tree analysis. *Research in Higher Education*, 45(3), 251–269.

Two Crows Corporation. (2005). *Introduction to data mining and knowledge discovery* (3rd ed.). Potomac, MD: Two Crows Corporation. Retrieved from http://www.twocrows. com/intro-dm.pdf

Vialardi, C., Bravo, J., Shafti, L., & Ortigosa, A. (2009). Recommendation in higher education using data mining techniques. In T. Barnes, M. Desmarais, C. Romero, & S. Ventura (Eds.), *Educational Data Mining 2009: 2nd International Conference on Educational Data Mining, Proceedings* (pp. 190–199). Cordoba, Spain: International Working Group on Educational Data Mining. Retrieved from http://www.educationaldatamining.org/EDM2009/uploads/proceedings/vialardi.pdf

Ware, M., Weissman, E., & McDermott, D. (2013). *Aid like a paycheck: Incremental aid to promote student success.* MDRC Policy Brief. New York, NY: MDRC. Retrieved from http://www.mdrc.org/sites/default/files/ALAP%20brief.pdf

Young, I. M. (1990). *Justice and the politics of difference.* Princeton, NJ: Princeton University Press.

JEFFREY ALAN JOHNSON *is the Interim Director of Institutional Effectiveness and Planning at Utah Valley University.*

8

Analytics derived from the student learning environment provide new insights into the collegiate experience; they can be used as a supplement to or, to some extent, in place of traditional surveys. To serve this purpose, however, greater attention must be paid to conceptual frameworks and to advancing institutional systems, activating new perspectives for practice.

Learning Analytics as a Counterpart to Surveys of Student Experience

Victor M. H. Borden, Hamish Coates

Surveys related to college student experience can be traced back to the early 20th century (Eells, 1937). Oversaturation of surveys and the attendant decline in response rates are only slightly more recent phenomena (Dey, 1997; Groves, 1989; Steeh, 1981). Advances in cost-effective methods for deploying surveys have exacerbated this problem, but surveys remain an important tool for higher education researchers and administrators to understand and work toward improving the student experience. The usefulness of student surveys is related closely to the practical interpretive frameworks upon which survey development has been based. However, critiques of these frameworks suggest that they are biased according to a limited range of student experience, especially given the growing diversity of student learners and learning environments (Museus, 2014). Learning analytics provide a potential source of new data related to the student experience that derives directly from current learning environments and learners. However, the atheoretical nature of approaches to analytics has constrained the use of data derived from learning analytics applications as indicators or measures of student experience. In this chapter, we trace the origins of the conceptual underpinnings of current popular student experience surveys and describe the results of a project that sought to bridge the gap between surveys and analytic approaches to assessing student experience.

The Student Survey Tradition

Surveys have a long, robust tradition as the primary vehicle for assessing the college student experience. In the first half of the 20th century, Eells (1937)

NEW DIRECTIONS FOR HIGHER EDUCATION, no. 179, Fall 2017 © 2017 Wiley Periodicals, Inc.
Published online in Wiley Online Library (wileyonlinelibrary.com) • DOI: 10.1002/he.20246

89

identified 240 student surveys in a review for the Carnegie Foundation for the Advancement of Teaching. In 1966, Astin and colleagues at the Higher Education Research Institute (HERI) of the University of California, Los Angeles, first administered the Freshman Survey as part of the Cooperative Institutional Research Program, a survey that is still popular 50 years later (Eagan et al., 2016). By the 1980s, theories of student integration (Spady, 1970; Tinto, 1975), student involvement (Astin, 1984), and student effort (Pace, 1982) spawned the development of such national instruments as the College Student Experience Questionnaire, as well as local campus surveys. National consulting organizations like the National Center for Higher Education Management Systems and Noel-Levitz utilized student surveys as a component of their consulting services. Around the turn of the millennium, the National Survey of Student Engagement (NSSE) was first administered, reflecting recent scholarship that focused attention on behavioral measures related to empirically established effective educational practices. Versions of the NSSE survey have since been deployed internationally as higher education institutions and national higher education policy agencies take a keener interest in student outcomes of the college experience (Coates & McCormick, 2014).

College campuses have long used surveys as part of their assessment and evaluation activities. In addition to the nationally (and now internationally) available instruments described above, many institutions have employed local surveys to assess satisfaction with programs and services, as well as the expectations of entering students and the behaviors of continuing students. Borden and Kernel (2012) describe the benefits and limitations of using local as compared to nationally available instruments. Local instruments provide users a greater degree of control and attention to local circumstances, along with the ability to develop common questions for surveys of different populations (for example, entering, continuing, and graduating students; alumni; faculty and staff). Although local instruments generally cost more (staff time) to develop, they can be more closely tied to local priorities. Despite their more generic focus, national surveys have the advantages of being developed by survey experts, validated across broader populations, and available for comparative benchmarks.

Advances in network and automated technologies have made surveys less expensive to conduct. Web-based survey platforms enable individuals with minimal technical (and survey development) expertise to put something together quickly and broadcast it widely. Even before the latest advancements, the ready availability and affordability of surveys have resulted in oversaturation and attendant declining response rates. Declining response rates have been noted since the latter part of the 20th century (Dey, 1997; Groves, 1989; Steeh, 1981), just as surveys began to play a central role in institutional research studies (Dey, 1997). Survey researchers have described various ways to address the challenges of modern survey research so as to improve data quality (Krosnick, Presser, Fealing, & Ruggles, 2015).

Table 8.2. Data Sources for Assessing the Nine Qualities of a Successful Student Experience

Quality	Associated Indicators	Data Availability
Discovery	Development of new technical, generic, and personal skills, advanced problem-solving skills, production of body of creative academic work; understanding academic culture and expectations; and acquisition of new interests.	Lagged data is available from national student and graduate surveys. There is a shortage of collected data that measures students' capacity for discovery; however, internal data points including curriculum and assessment systems, and commercial online profiling platforms would yield richer information.
Achievement	Admission, passing, retention, learning outcomes, completion, and articulation into other qualifications.	Lagged data is available from national student surveys and data collections, state-based admissions agencies. Additional information could be harnessed through e-portfolios or tracking mechanisms. There is a shortage of publicly available information on learning outcomes.
Opportunity	Awareness of career opportunities and strategies, further study readiness, graduate, employment, participating in collaborative networks, and participating in experiential learning or in leadership roles.	Lagged data is available from national student, graduate, and employer surveys. Additional information could be gained from admission agencies and institutional alumni information and systems. There is a shortage of collected data that measures opportunities seized by individual students; however, participation in institutional events, leadership roles, experiential activities, and graduate outcomes could be logged.
Value	Graduate outcomes, course fees, course duration, work experience opportunities, physical and online facilities and services, perceptions of teacher quality, identification of study purpose aspirations, and student information.	Lagged data is available from national student, graduate, and employer surveys. Additional information could be gained from student service use and incidence of attendance, exit interviews, institutional alumni systems, and social media platforms.

(Continued)

Table 8.2. Continued

Quality	Associated Indicators	Data Availability
Connection	Exposure to industry events, speakers, and networks; undertaking work placements; student exchange and volunteering; and forming academic, collegial, and social networks.	Lagged data is available from national student surveys. Additional information could be gained from institutional systems, work integrated learning experiences, online discussion boards, interaction in student groups, and commercial networks used in course work. New collections that log student attendance or participation in industry or academic events. Subscriptions, membership, and participation in professional or academic networking platforms, organizations, and chat rooms would indicate connectedness.
Belonging	Feeling welcomed; awareness and participation in groups, forums, and clubs; participation in online and face-to-face curricular and noncurricular activities; and forming and maintaining relationships.	Lagged data is available from national student and graduate surveys. Additional institutional systems that log participation, attendance, and duration of experience on campus or online could be used in conjunction with records that indicate attendance at orientation events, and membership and participation in groups. Other new forms of data could include real-time student feedback about perceptions or swipe card data. Alumni information and commercial online profiling offer other data.
Personalized	Staff engagement with students, tailoring curriculum and teaching to students, experience/advice that is tailored to individuals, and provision of real-time assessment.	Data is available, or could be made available, from national student surveys and institution systems on the extent to which staff and infrastructure are personalized. There is more information available on commercial platforms.

(Continued)

Table 8.2. Continued

Quality	Associated Indicators	Data Availability
Enabled	Student aid, scholarship availability, teacher quality, assessment feedback, academic support, online and physical resources, and student development sessions.	Lagged data is available from national student and graduate surveys. Information from tertiary admission centers and institutional scholarship data could be used. Additional institutional systems that record incidence of support services, attendance at noncompulsory curricular events, and use of online and physical resources including careers advice or utilization of digital systems would provide information. Institutional information about alumni and commercial online profiling offer other data sources.
Identity	Leadership skills, cultural awareness, emotional intelligence, self-reflectiveness.	Lagged data is available from national student and graduate surveys. Institutional systems including administrative data and others that house assessment items including reflective and practical journals, capstone experiences, and exchanges. Data that identifies participation in mentoring, leadership, or orientation events or peer assisted programs. Information about student awards and recognition and volunteer roles for both curricular and noncurricular activities could be captured. Other commercial online systems or personal blogs offer additional data sources.

"intersectionality" (Dill & Zambrana, 2009), which forwards an approach to identity that uses intersecting vectors of relevant information to account for differences in identity criteria, to build complex pictures of who people are. Such identity delineation already abounds for anyone with an online presence, yet is just starting to emerge in higher education. Taking this approach helps move beyond bundling people into simplistic groups/boxes that fail to provide the nuance necessary for helping individuals succeed.

The ideas of profiles and journeys are useful tools for conveying this approach. Simply put, a profile can be envisaged as a complex dynamic of diverse attributes that portray an individual in relation to a successful student experience. A journey is a multiple branching pathway through

a higher education process, from beginning to end. The idea of profil-
ing "movements through journeys" steps well beyond the idea of shifting
"batched groups through lifecycles." Together these two approaches may
seem at first glance to unleash infinite complexity for conceptualizing and
managing each student's experience, but the history in other industries im-
plies otherwise. After initial reworking in terms of new processes, effective
digitization in the commercial services and products sector has been shown
to yield substantial increases in productivity and quality of people's purposeful interactions with organizations (Bommel, Edelman, & Ungerman,
2014).

   Figure 8.1 depicts how such information might be relayed in a sample
student success report. For each quality it presents information (scored on
a scale ranging from 1 to 10) for students in a course (major), an individual
student's success to date, and individual expectations. Different actors will
of course interface with this information in different ways. Indeed, understanding differences in perspectives and interpretation has proved to be an
important part of how new forms of data are being positioned and developed in traditional, existing higher education structures (which are often
changing themselves). It is important to design new approaches that take
very seriously the demands of consequential validity. Technical development can then be driven by a clear sense of what should be achieved. The
approach enacted in this study—involving reviews and discussions about
research and practice—has sought to design an approach that yields meaningful insights for key stakeholders such as students, teachers, support staff,
managers, leaders, and the public at large.

   The Australian study was guided by the important rationale and
premise that there is a pressing need for collaborative research and development of student experience, data, and leadership. Pushing ahead separately
on each of these frontiers will not achieve the desired change. Rather, leadership must focus more on using data for student success, data must be
more aligned with student success and relevant to leaders, and student success must be grounded in data and leadership. Finding a sweet spot that
unites data with experience with leadership carries valuable potential for
improving higher education.

   The study's research and consultation clarified aspects of data-informed
leadership. In higher education, leadership is invariably a distributed activity that involves a wide variety of people and certainly not just people in
formal management roles. In particular, and somewhat obviously, students
play an enormously important role in cocreating a successful experience.
Improving student success hinges on staff and student leaders using data to
understand and steer practice. Data-informed leadership of student success
is impossible if data does not exist, is not collated or reported in meaningful ways, or is not focused on the qualities that matter for student success.
Work on successful experience must be articulated and also underpinned
by a suitable evidence base that is reported in ways relevant to people with

Figure 8.1. Sample Student Success Report

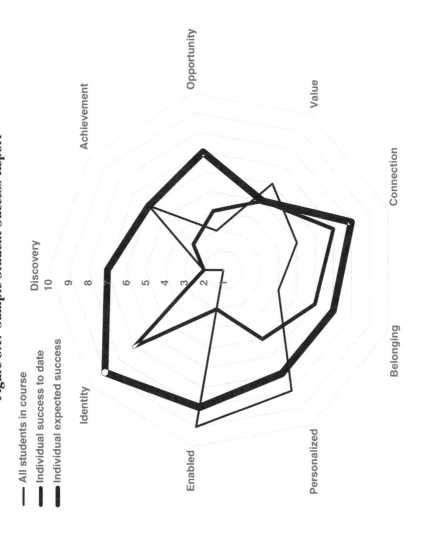

— All students in course
▮ Individual success to date
▮ Individual expected success

Discovery

10
9
8
6
5
4
3
2
1

Opportunity

Achievement

Value

Connection

Identity

Belonging

Enabled

Personalized

the capacity to shape change, including individual instructors and students themselves.

Conclusions and Implications

We suggest in this chapter that student analytics provides a promising technique for assessing student experience at the individual level, while still providing a more general view of important shared dimensions among the student body of an institution of higher education and the higher education sector more broadly. To serve these purposes, we must break away from some of the traditional assumptions about learners and their experience but, at the same time, preserve the strong interpretative scaffolding that well-constructed concepts and theories provide in comparison to atheoretical, predictive models. Knowing precisely how likely a student is to pass or fail does not provide actionable information on how to help any student. It is critical to understand *why* the student is not performing up to par, as well as how to constructively intervene. In addition, generalizing experience to a whole demographic segment based on a group mean of a proxy indicator of experience does not serve any student well and may preserve existing biases. Our theories about student experience must therefore include consideration of cultural biases, institutionalized biases, and the power relationships inherent in the teaching and learning environment that perpetuate these biases.

The research and theory that guided the development of seminal concepts of student experience, like engagement, integration, and involvement, were shaped primarily by an idealized residential student experience for college-age, primarily White students at U.S. colleges and universities, during a period of history in which a college education was becoming increasingly seen as the ticket to a job or career that would provide more than just a living wage. It is impossible to investigate student experience without recognizing that the world has changed. As higher education changes, so too have institutional responses to engaging students (van der Velden, 2012). The massification of higher education (Marope, Wells, & Hazelkorn, 2013; OECD, 2009), the impact of technological innovation, the increase in student diversity in higher education, and a dramatic change in social success and employment prospects for graduates have together created new dynamics for student experience. The considerable investment of time and resources, which is often accompanied by the perspective of significant debt, undermines students' motivation for excellence and engagement.

We may well need new thinking and conceptualization about the student experience, such as the nine qualities model. Another useful construct that we need to consider is intersectionality (Crenshaw, 1989). Rather than viewing students as belonging to one group or another, we need to understand that each student's identity is a unique composite of the socially constructed identities related indirectly to such demographic characteristics as gender, race, ethnicity, religion, regional origin, and so on. These approaches can support theoretically framed approaches to understanding and hence managing student profiles and journeys. The advent of student analytics provides an opportunity for us to break away from outmoded thought, but it does not obviate the need for theories to guide practice. Student analytics can stimulate the development of new, more relevant models of student experience that have the role of learning and development in shaping the future life of students individually and collectively.

References

Arnold, K. E., Lonn, S., & Pistilli, M. D. (2014). An exercise in institutional reflection: The learning analytics readiness instrument (LARI). In A. Pardo & S. Teasley (Eds.), *Proceedings from the Fourth International Conference on Learning Analytics and Knowledge* (pp. 163–167). New York, NY: ACM. https://doi.org/10.1145/2567574.2567621

Astin, A. W. (1984). Student involvement: A developmental theory for higher education. *Journal of College Student Personnel, 25*(4), 297–308.

Bommel, E., Edelman, D., & Ungerman, K. (2014). Digitizing the consumer decision journey. *McKinsey Quarterly.* Retrieved from http://www.mckinsey.com/business-fun ctions/marketing-and-sales/our-insights/digitizing-the-consumer-decision-journey

Borden, V. M. H. (2004). Accommodating student swirl. *Change: The Magazine of Higher Education, 36*(2), 10–17.

Borden, V. M. H., & Kernel, B. (2012). *Measuring quality: Guidelines.* Website resource cosponsored by the Association for Institutional Research, the American Council on Education, and the National Institute for Learning Outcomes Assessment. Retrieved from http://apps.airweb.org/surveys/Guidelines.aspx

Coates, H., & Ainley, J. (2007). *Graduates course experience 2007: The report of the course experience questionnaire (CEQ).* Carlton, VIC: GCA.

Coates, H., Kelly, P., Naylor, R., & Borden, V. (2017). *Innovative approaches for enhancing the 21st century student experience.* Canberra: Department of Education and Training.

Coates, H., & McCormick, A. C. (2014). Introduction: Student engagement—A window into undergraduate education. In H. Coates & A. C. McCormick (Eds.), *Engaging university students: International insights from system-wide studies* (pp. 1–12). Singapore: Springer.

Crenshaw, K. (1989). Demarginalizing the intersection of race and sex: A black feminist critique of antidiscrimination doctrine, feminist theory and antiracist politics. *University of Chicago Legal Forum, 140,* 139–167.

Dey, E. L. (1997). Working with low survey response rates: The efficacy of weighting adjustments. *Research in Higher Education, 38*(2), 215–227.

Dill, B. T., & Zambrana, R. E. (2009). *Emerging intersections: Race, class, and gender in theory, policy, and practice.* New Brunswick, NJ: Rutgers University Press.

Eagan, M. K., Stolzenberg, E. B., Ramirez, J. J., Aragon, M. C., Suchard, M. R., & Rios-Aguilar, C. (2016). *The American freshman: Fifty-year trends, 1966–2015.* Los Angeles, CA: Higher Education Research Institute, UCLA.

Eells, W. C. (1937). *Surveys of American higher education.* New York, NY: Carnegie Foundation for the Advancement of Teaching.

Groves, R. M. (1989). *Survey errors and survey costs.* New York, NY: Wiley.

Krosnick, J. A., Presser, S., Fealing, K. H., & Ruggles, S. (2015). *The future of survey research: Challenges and opportunities.* National Science Foundation Advisory Committee for the Social, Behavioral and Economic Sciences Subcommittee on Advancing SBE Survey Research. Retrieved from https://www.nsf.gov/sbe/AC_Materials/The_Future_of_Survey_Research.pdf

Marope, P. T. M., Wells, P. J., & Hazelkorn, E. (Eds.). (2013). *Rankings and accountability in higher education: Uses and misuses.* Paris: UNESCO.

McCormick, A. C. (2003). Swirling and double-dipping: New patterns of student attendance and their implications for higher education. In J. E. King, E. L. Anderson, and M. E. Corrigan (Eds.), *Changing student attendance patterns: Challenges for policy and practice, New Directions for Higher Education, No. 121* (pp. 13–24). San Francisco, CA: Jossey-Bass.

Museus, S. D. (2014). The Culturally Engaging Campus Environments (CECE) Model: A new theory of success among racially diverse college student populations. In M. B. Paulsen (Ed.), *Higher education: Handbook of theory and research* (pp. 189–227). New York, NY: Springer.

OECD. (2009). *Higher education to 2030—Volume 2: Globalisation.* Paris: OECD Publishing. Retrieved from http://www.oecd.org/edu/ceri/highereducationto2030volume2globalisation.htm

Pace, C. R. (1982). *Achievement and the quality of student effort.* Los Angeles: University of California, Higher Education Research Institute, Graduate School of Education.

Pistilli, M. D., Willis, J. E., III, & Campbell, J. P. (2014). Analytics through an institutional lens: Definition, theory, design, and impact. In J. A. Larusson & B. White (Eds.), *Learning analytics: From research to practice* (pp. 79–101). New York, NY: Springer.

Spady, W. G. (1970). Dropouts from higher education: An interdisciplinary review and synthesis. *Interchange, 1,* 64–85.

Steeh, C. J. (1981). Trends in nonresponse rates. *Public Opinion Quarterly, 45,* 40–57.

Tinto, V. (1975). Dropout from higher education: A theoretical synthesis of recent research. *Review of Educational Research, 45*(1), 89–125.

van der Velden, G. (2012), Institutional level student engagement and organisational cultures. *Higher Education Quarterly, 66,* 227–247.

DR. VICTOR BORDEN *is a Professor of Higher Education within the Department of Educational Leadership and Policy Studies at Indiana University Bloomington.*

DR. HAMISH COATES *is a Professor of Higher Education at the University of Melbourne's Centre for the Study of Higher Education (CSHE).*

analytics generated feedback can be provided to students, and how students' use of that information can be tracked to better understand the value of feedback. The authors of Chapter 2 demonstrate how the work at Stanford University focuses on digital behaviors related to content and skill mastery and further underscores the importance of approaching this work as part of a cycle of inquiry-based continuous improvement. A few more broad questions that leaders need to grapple with are, "What are analytics telling us?" and "What are we trying to create?" The author of Chapter 7 warns against ethical issues related to user privacy, while also challenging readers to think about the inferences made about individuals captured within learning analytics systems. Meanwhile, the authors of Chapter 5 describe several strategies (for example, colloquium, task force, and grant opportunities) for fostering a broad concept of what learning analytics can look like. Interrogating these broad questions—*how*, *why*, and *what*—allows leaders not only to articulate a clear vision of learning analytics on their campus, but also to engage in these projects as part of a broader culture of inquiry that fosters organizational learning and development.

Social Justice

Inequities within higher education can either be addressed, continued, or exacerbated by the use of learning analytics. An important aspect found within the Mount St. Mary's University example cited in this volume was how the university president planned to use data predicting student failure. This case prompts ethical questions such as, "Is it right for an institution to accept students who are predicted to fail?" or, more importantly, "Doesn't an institution have the responsibility to provide needed support to the students it admits and charges tuition?" In Chapter 7, the author's emphasis on continued structural justice, the establishment of systems that promote and the dismantling of systems that impede actions of self-development and self-determination, is a critical and guiding principle in learning analytics development. A particular example of this can be found in Chapter 3, where the authors discuss the tension between the request of faculty who wanted to learn if students had been flagged in classes beyond their own and the ultimate decision not to acquiesce to this request, for fear of the ways this access would impede student development. Adding to these considerations is the examination of the student role in learning analytics, as provided in Chapter 6, where the author describes how learning analytics can be used as a signaling device for students who may be unaware of the need to, but are motivated to, improve their learning and success. Ethical considerations related to this aspect of learning analytics include, "To what extent should the results of learning analytics be turned over to students with varying degrees of digital literacy?" and "How can we create systems that empower, instead of impede, students' own role in their success?" The examination of the student's role was not limited to the sixth chapter, as many authors commented on the degree of independence afforded to the student when designing learning analytics.

Returning to the quotation opening this chapter, it is our hope that readers of this volume refocus their energy toward crucial aspects of learning analytics. Far too often, we've observed institutions that purchase a technology hoping that it, alone, will solve institutional problems or departments pour resources into developing algorithms to predict student success, without any intent of understanding why students are at risk and how they can best be supported and provided agency for their own learning. The demands of learning analytics highlighted in this volume regarding organizational structures, values, and behaviors are not easy "add-ons" to be clarified by the introduction of some tool. Instead, learning analytics is a way to reshape these components within a higher education system and empower stakeholders dedicated to realizing the goals of this enterprise.

Reference

Kelley, E. C. (1951). *The workshop way of learning*. New York, NY: Harper.

DR. JOHN ZILVINSKIS *is an Assistant Professor of Student Affairs Administration at Binghamton University - State University of New York (SUNY).*

DR. VICTOR BORDEN *is a Professor of Higher Education within the Department of Educational Leadership and Policy Studies at Indiana University Bloomington.*

INDEX

SAY HELLO TO YOUR INCOMING CLASS
THEY'RE NOT MILLENNIALS ANYMORE

"[A] groundbreaking study [that] provides leaders at all levels the understanding of today's student that is critical to creating the conditions that help students thrive."
— DR. KEITH HUMPHREY, vice president for student affairs, and past president, ACPA–College Student Educators International

"Already, it has accelerated my getting acquainted with Generation Z in our work on college campuses. The data is first, fresh and insightful."
— DR. TIM ELMORE, president, GrowingLeaders.com

"[A] refreshing, straight-forward and optimistic portrayal of today's college student [that] will change how educators develop, empower and relate to them."
— NANCY HUNTER DENNEY, executive director, Lead365 National Conference

COREY SEEMILLER
MEGHAN GRACE

GENERATION Z GOES TO COLLEGE

JB JOSSEY-BASS™
A Wiley Brand

"Timely and relevant... the book is a must-read for any college student educator!**"**
— DR. PAIGE HABER-CURRAN, assistant professor, Texas State University

Generation Z is rapidly replacing Millennials on college campuses. Those born 1995–2010 have different motivations, learning styles, characteristics, skill sets, and social concerns than previous generations. Unlike Millennials, these students grew up in a recession and are under few illusions. *Generation Z Goes to College* is the first book on how this up-and-coming generation will change higher education, reporting findings from an in-depth study of over 1,100 college students from 15 vastly different higher education institutions.

FIND OUT WHAT YOUR NEXT INCOMING CLASS IS ALL ABOUT.

JB JOSSEY-BASS
A Wiley Brand

NEW DIRECTIONS FOR HIGHER EDUCATION

ORDER FORM SUBSCRIPTION AND SINGLE ISSUES

DISCOUNTED BACK ISSUES:

Use this form to receive 20% off all back issues of *New Directions for Higher Education*.
All single issues priced at **$23.20** (normally $29.00)

TITLE	ISSUE NO.	ISBN

Call 1-800-835-6770 or see mailing instructions below. When calling, mention the promotional code JBNND to receive your discount. For a complete list of issues, please visit www.wiley.com/WileyCDA/WileyTitle/productCd-HE.html

SUBSCRIPTIONS: (1 YEAR, 4 ISSUES)

☐ New Order   ☐ Renewal

U.S.	☐ Individual: $89	☐ Institutional: $356
CANADA/MEXICO	☐ Individual: $89	☐ Institutional: $398
ALL OTHERS	☐ Individual: $113	☐ Institutional: $434

Call 1-800-835-6770 or see mailing and pricing instructions below.
Online subscriptions are available at www.onlinelibrary.wiley.com

ORDER TOTALS:

Issue / Subscription Amount: $ _____

Shipping Amount: $ _____
(for single issues only – subscription prices include shipping)

Total Amount: $ _____

SHIPPING CHARGES:
First Item $6.00
Each Add'l Item $2.00

(No sales tax for U.S. subscriptions. Canadian residents, add GST for subscription orders. Individual rate subscriptions must be paid by personal check or credit card. Individual rate subscriptions may not be resold as library copies.)

BILLING & SHIPPING INFORMATION:

☐ **PAYMENT ENCLOSED:** *(U.S. check or money order only. All payments must be in U.S. dollars.)*

☐ **CREDIT CARD:** ☐ VISA ☐ MC ☐ AMEX

Card number _____Exp. Date_____

Card Holder Name_____Card Issue # _____

Signature _____Day Phone_____

☐ **BILL ME:** *(U.S. institutional orders only. Purchase order required.)*

Purchase order # _____
Federal Tax ID 13559302 • GST 89102-8052

Name_____

Address_____

Phone_____ E-mail_____

Copy or detach page and send to: **John Wiley & Sons, Inc. / Jossey Bass**
PO Box 55381
Boston, MA 02205-9850

PROMO JBNND